I had this idea that I was going to rope a deer, put it in a stall, feed it up on corn for a couple of weeks, then kill it and eat it. The first step in this adventure was getting a deer. I figured that, since they congregate at my cattle feeder and do not seem to have much fear of me when we are there (a bold one will sometimes come right up and sniff at the bags of feed while I am in the back of the truck not 4 feet away), it should not be difficult to rope one, get up to it and toss a bag over its head (to calm it down) then hog tie it and transport it home.

I filled the cattle feeder then hid down at the end with my rope. The cattle, having seen the roping thing before, stayed well back. They were not having any of it. After about 20 minutes, three deer showed up.

I picked out a likely looking one, stepped out from the end of the feeder, and threw my rope. The deer just stood there and stared at me. I wrapped the rope around my waist and twisted the end so I would have a good hold. The deer still just stood and stared at me, but you could tell it was mildly concerned about the whole rope situation. I took a step towards it...it took a step away. I put a little tension on the rope and then I received an education.

The first thing that I learned is that, while a deer may just stand there looking at you funny while you rope it, they are spurred to action when you start pulling on that rope. That deer EXPLODED.

The second thing I learned is that pound for pound, a deer is a LOT stronger than a cow or a colt. A cow or a colt in that weight range I could fight down with a rope and with some dignity. A deer? no chance. That thing ran and bucked and twisted and pulled. There was no controlling it and certainly no getting close to it. As it jerked me off my feet and started dragging me across the ground, it occurred to me that having a deer on a rope was not nearly as good an idea as I had originally imagined...

(Excerpted from Chapter 12, "Barry and the Deer.")

To my grandchildren, Olivia, Julia, Malcolm, and Sophie

BLUEBIRDS
TO TIKAL

Stories of fun, fear, & folly

Also by David Hann

The Jayhawker Cleveland
2021, Anamcara Press.

"The Deer on the Fence"
Living Now magazine, (from *River Memoir*)

"Sailors on a Sea of Grass"
Oskaloosa Independent (from *Sampling Kansas*)

"The Ballad of Jake Brakes"
Lawrence Journal World, Chanute Tribune, The Great American Poetry Show, Vol. 3, 2015

Sampling Kansas: A Guide to the Curious
Kansas Past: Pieces of the 34th, Star Penthe Press

River Memoir and Other Stories

BLUEBIRDS TO TIKAL

Stories of fun, fear, & folly

DAVID HANN

Anamcara Press LLC

Published in 2023 by Anamcara Press LLC

Author © 2023 by David Hann
Cover & Book design by Maureen Carroll
Deer photo by Ronda Miller
Adobe Caslon Pro, Tsisquilisda, Berlin Sans FB
Printed in the United States of America.

Book Description: Discover why deer don't like to be lassoed, what it's like to drive down a mountain pass without power steering or power brakes after the engine quits, and learn what can happen when cultures clash in these stories of fun, fear, and folly.

ANAMCARA PRESS LLC
P.O. Box 442072, Lawrence, KS 66044
https://anamcara-press.com/

Ordering Information:
Quantity sales. Special discounts are available on quantity purchases by corporations, associations, and others. For details, contact the publisher at the address above.
Orders by U.S. trade bookstores and wholesalers. Please contact Ingram Distribution.

ISBN-13: 978-1-960462-03-9 eBook
ISBN-13: 978-1-960462-02-2 hardback
ISBN-13: 978-1-960462-01-5 paperback

NAT024000	NATURE / Essays
HUM022000	HUMOR / Topic / History
HUM026000	HUMOR / Topic / Travel
HIS027070	HISTORY / Wars & Conflicts / Vietnam War
HIS036090	HISTORY / United States / State & Local / Midwest
BIO023000	BIOGRAPHY & AUTOBIOGRAPHY / Adventurers & Explorers

Library of Congress Control Number: 2023935648

CONTENTS

INTRODUCTION

These stories are written to entertain. They may be informative, amusing, scary, even thought provoking. The twenty-three stories fall into four groups: travel stories, stories told to me, Marine Corps stories, and some other adventures.

A family traveling to Guatemala to see the Mayan ruins at Tikal encounters "los hombres militares" and uniformed soldiers. A sightseeing trip in Turkey meets with obstacles, courtesy, and help from an unexpected source. Culture clash and exotic sites were the norm in Central Asia. What was supposed to be an idyllic kayak vacation in Florida turns into something quite different. A visit to the Eiffel Tower ends with eviction by security guards. Riding the rails before World War I presents adventure and danger for two young men searching for jobs as they make their way through the Northwest. Army medics assigned to anti-aircraft gunners on a destroyer in WW II find themselves in a precarious position when German fighters attack their ship. Two young Army men in WW I exact a kind of revenge after being conned into attending a religious revival. A kindly foreman is invited to the east Arkansas backwoods by two grateful employees. Watching an eighteen-month old baby girl turns out to be not as easy as the sitter was led to believe. Two young girls in western Kansas encounter the Jackrabbit Man. Some students from Central Asia see some buffalo and a mountain lion cub, up close. A newly hired college graduate finds that prejudice comes in many guises. A friend finds out, painfully, that deer don't like to be lassoed. What is it like to drive down a mountain pass without power steering or power brakes after the engine quits? A retired coal miner recounts his life in the mines of Osage County, Kansas. Two German noblewomen compete for the affections of a dashing cavalry officer

And more stories of fun, fear, and folly.

David Hann

PART I -
TRAVEL STORIES

Chapter 1

BLUEBIRDS TO TIKAL

One Guatemalan soldier patted me down as I stood feet and hands spread apart, my face pressed against the Bluebird bus. Another soldier held his automatic rifle at my back while my wife, Rose, and daughters Sarah and Rachel watched. This was the third time in two days armed men had ordered us off our bus at gunpoint.

I used my limited Spanish to explain we had been to Tikal to see the ruins. The young soldier nodded and continued patting me down. From the corner of my eye I saw the rifle begin to slip from his shoulder and cartwheel down to the ground. I thought, "If he doesn't have his safety on and has a round in the chamber the rifle will fire and the other soldier will shoot me out of reflex." All this action and thought took place in the seconds it took for the rifle to strike earth. No shot. Okay so far.

The soldier re-slung his rifle and said, "Okay." I looked over my shoulder and the man with the gun at my back gestured with the point of his rifle to rejoin the other bus passengers.

As we waited to re-board our bus I recalled what John said two days ago in Belize City, where we had fled from a frigid Kansas winter to tropical Belize, planning to travel in Guatemala before returning to Belize to celebrate Christmas 1983 on the island of Caye Cauker.

"Don't go. You can't fly into Tikal. It's only been a few months since the military coup. Army or guerillas burned down the control tower."

"We want to take the girls and see the Mayan ruins around Tikal," Rose said.

John shook his head.

"You will have to take buses to Tikal and the roads might not be reliable."

"What do you mean, not reliable?" Rose asked.

John shrugged. "Maybe dangerous. There may still be some guerilla activity, or maybe the army will be checking the buses."

"We're going," said Rose.

Well, John was right. Yesterday and earlier today, it was "los hombres militares," armed men in peasant clothing who ordered us off the bus. We didn't know on whose side the armed civilians were, not that it mattered. Now it was uniformed soldiers, pro-government I assumed.

Our Guatemala trip had begun yesterday in Belize City on one of the Beatty Bus Company's fleet of aging Bluebird buses. When we reached the Guatemalan border the immigration officer informed us that we didn't have proper papers to enter the country. The officer looked to me like he was suffering from a hangover and was not in a good mood.

I wanted to pay the bribe and obtain the "proper papers" but Rose would have none of it because we had purchased visas for Guatemala. She opened my Spanish phrase book, scanned it, then pointed to herself and said "advocate," meaning lawyer. I could tell this didn't sit well with the man and I began to wonder what it would be like spending some time in a Guatemalan jail. Finally, after much arguing between Rose, myself, and the border control officer we obtained different papers from him for a small fee, about $3 apiece.

We stayed our first night in Guatemala in the border town of Melchor de Menos at the Hotel Zacalejo. After a short sleep punctuated by firecrackers, cats yowling and a drunk retching loudly outside our window, we boarded another Bluebird bus at 3 a.m. The driver's cassette player blasted Spanish dance music. The road, rough as a dry streambed, pitched and rolled us against the unyielding metal seats.

At one stop, a young woman holding a baby got on. Because all seats were taken, I stood up and offered my seat to her. She sat down. I was surprised when each of the Indians who got on with her stepped over and shook my hand.

The morning was still dark when we heard the word Cruce and tried to get off thinking that was our place, Las Cruces. The rest of the passengers stopped us, saying "Malo," or "Falta." We didn't need to understand Spanish to know that was a bad place to get off and wait for a bus.

Bus headlights blinked off and on frequently and sometimes, the times for which I was most grateful, the booming cassette player shut down too. No matter, the driver pressed ahead in the darkness and the bus tumbled on, like a huge firefly blinking its message. We slid to a sudden stop. I looked out the front windshield and saw we had startled a white horse standing asleep in the road. The half-awake horse lurched off to the side and our bus rumbled off into the darkness.

We reached Las Cruces just at dawn and waited for an hour or so before boarding the Tikal-bound bus. Sarah and Rachel and Rose found seats. I stood and nodded to the other passengers. Some of them ignored me. Some nodded back and I conversed with a few of them best we could with my butchering of Spanish. I enjoyed pulling out my dictionary and explaining to people about Kansas and its wheat and prairie and that my great grandfather had been a Texas cowboy who settled in Kansas. It seemed like everyone had heard about Texas and knew what a cowboy was.

I was turned towards the back of the bus talking with a deaf teacher of deaf children who could read my lips. The bus slowed down and stopped. She looked past me and said, "Hombres militares."

I turned and saw armed men wearing loose white trousers and white shirts standing behind a simple barricade, a log on a swivel they swung around to block the road. They carried rifles or shotguns. More men stood off to either side of the barrier. People got out of the bus. I told Rose that maybe we should stay in the bus. Seconds later one of the armed men poked his head in and said, "Todos." We got out and stood around with the others.

I thought that the Indians who had gotten onto the bus with shotguns, even though they were broken down, would be detained or at least have their shotguns taken from them. No such thing. The guerillas or whoever they were, were very polite and businesslike. They sent us on our way without any threat that I could see, other than their weapons loosely pointed at us, and their expressionless faces.

We managed to get to the Jaguar Inn at Tikal in time for supper and an embarrassing moment for me after dinner. Rose and the girls had left the restaurant and, alone with the young woman cashier, I pulled out some large bills and said, "Puede caminar?" Her eyes flashed and narrowed in anger. Then I realized I had effectively propositioned her by showing money and asking her if she wanted to go for a walk (caminar) instead of asking her if she could make change (cambiar). I corrected myself "Lo siento. Equivicado. Puede cambiar?" saying (I hoped) "Sorry. Mistake. Can you make change?" She laughed then and changed my large bills into smaller ones.

We went to bed immediately after dinner because we had to get up before dawn to walk to the ruins. We chatted a bit about our adventurous day, especially our encounter with "los hombres militares."

"Not likely to happen again," I assured Rose and the girls.

With these optimistic thoughts I drifted off to sleep. Lizards ran along the ceiling rafters and both they and insects dropped onto our mosquito nets. That didn't bother me or Rose but the girls slept fitfully. In the morning we had to step over a long corridor of army ants whose legions stretched back into the jungle.

We hiked along a well-worn jungle trail to the Temple of the Jaguar. Oldest daughter Sarah spooked younger sister Rachel with tales of crocodiles lurking in the bush. Rachel countered with more plausible tales of poisonous snakes because Sarah feared snakes more than anything. The girls frightened one another so much they declared a truce.

Fortunately, we reached the Temple of the Jaguar and the one opposite it, the Temple of the Masks, with no reptile encounters. Both temples, dating from the early 700s, rose more than 150 feet from the jungle and had been so overgrown they were not discovered until 1962, just twenty-one years before we got there.

I scrambled up the short-rise steps on the Temple of the Masks so that I could photograph the Jaguar Temple. Park rangers had installed a chain running to the top for cautious people like me to use. One slip on those steps could bring a painful, maybe fatal roll to the bottom of the stone structure, which is why Rose forbade the girls to climb up. John had told us that he couldn't return to Tikal for awhile because last time he was there, without a pass, a park ranger had chased our fleet-footed friend up the Temple of the Masks, slipped, and rolled down the steps and broke his leg.

We returned from the ruins just in time to catch a bus to make our way back to Belize. A few minutes later los hombres militares stopped us. Armed men, some not looking much older than 13-year-old Sarah, ordered us off the bus and searched through everyone's papers. One of the younger ones tarried looking through 10-year-old Rachel's book, an illustrated copy of *Wind in the Willows*. A sharp command from an older man snapped him out of his reverie.

I looked away from the searching and noticed six low-flying Canada Geese. Without thinking I exclaimed, "Mira!" Everyone stopped to gaze at the big birds as they flew just fifty or so feet above us. The guerillas completed searching and we continued on our way to our third and last encounter with armed men in Guatemala.

After the Guardia National, or whoever they were, finished their business we boarded the bus and returned to Belize City, where we took a taxi to Mama's Restaurant. Two men brawled in a fistfight just outside the restaurant entrance. Belize City was a pretty wild town.

I escorted Rose and the girls past the combatants and found a table for them inside. "I'll try to find someone to take us out to the island." Rose and the girls were grateful to sit down and have the gracious Mama attend to them while I went to search along the waterfront.

There I met a young man, Jerome, who answered my queries about my friend, John, and Caye Cauker by saying that he knew John and was just about ready to head for the island. He only needed to pick up two friends who also lived on Caye Cauker. The young men, Angel and Gregorio, joined us. Gregorio lightly clutched his stomach. Jerome explained.

"He got stabbed in the stomach during a fight and had to get stitched up at the hospital."

Angel had a thin scar running down one side of his face, another knife fight I presumed. I got into the boat.

The estuary to the sea ran behind some hotels and Mama's Restaurant. When I hopped out and told Rose I had a ride to the island, she was skeptical. "Mama told me to be careful because there are two men who say they will take you out, then take your money and leave you on a mangrove island."

John explained when we first arrived there that Belize City had become so ungovernable that the nation of Belize moved the official capitol inland from Belize City to Belmopan. John asked, "What do you expect from a country that was founded by pirates?"

So I told Jerome that I wanted to speak with Danny Weir, who owned the Bel Cove Hotel, where we had spent the night before our exciting Guatemala adventure. I yelled up to Danny and asked him if these guys were all right. Danny gazed down at them from a hotel balcony and rubbed his unshaven chin while mulling over my query.

"W-e-l-l, I guess so."

Not a ringing endorsement but we needed to head out now to arrive at Caye Cauker before nightfall. I nodded to Jerome and as the sky darkened we headed out to Caye Cauker with three young men descended from pirates, the warning from Mama echoing.

Partly because of the need to get to Caye Cauker before dark and partly because he wanted to show off his boat's prowess, Jerome sped into the chop. The boat pounded the waves. We sat on the thwarts at the front of the boat getting pounded by the impact of the boat hitting the chop. I kept my gaze directed towards the three young men in the back. Jerome stood and later I found this was the best way to ride, so that one's legs absorbed the shock rather than the spine.

We ran into a chubasco, a short rain squall, and that plus the fact that Gregorio's knife wound was beginning to bleed again prompted Jerome to ask if we could pull over to a mangrove island to wait out the squall—just what Rose had been warned about. Rose and I vigorously shook our heads.

"No, let's keep going. Want to be there before dark." The rain pelted us. We pushed our bags into a space under the prow, hoping to shield them from the rain. Rachel and Sarah burrowed under the prow with the bags. It looked to me like they were laughing hysterically.

Jerome shrugged and we pounded our way through the chop to Caye Cauker. Later John told me that Jerome, Angel and Gregorio said I was like a crazy man for insisting to power through the rain squall. "He just wanted to keep going," complained Jerome, shaking his head.

✸ ✸ ✸

We read in the news after our trip that an American tourist had been shot and killed when he tried to run a roadblock set up by one of the combatants in the civil war; whether the guerillas or their counterparts, it didn't say. Rose felt bad that her enthusiasm for taking the girls to Tikal put us all in danger, but home safe we only remembered the fun parts.

Chapter 2

FLAT TIRE IN TURKEY

Storm clouds threatened rain, causing us to end our swim in the Mediterranean Sea off Side, Turkey. It was the last day of May, and very warm, so we didn't mind standing by the road with our wet hair waiting for a bus to come along. Mubeccel, Rose and I were returning to our hotel in Antalya. Mubeccel, our long-time friend, Turkish language teacher and travel companion, explained that a bus would stop fairly soon.

Rose, with her dark hair and small stature, similar to Mubeccel, could have passed for a Turkish woman. Rose could speak Turkish fairly well whereas I stumbled along as best I could, finding most Turks patient and even grateful at my attempts to speak their language. My blue eyes, faltering speech and generally Western appearance revealed to casual observers that I was American. Fortunately, Turks like Americans even though they, like me, might not always agree with my country's politics.

The young man who was the bus conductor noticed our wet hair and asked out of curiosity why our hair was wet. "Had we been to a Hamam (Turkish bath)?" We explained that we had been swimming at a beach in Side, but a storm blew in just when we got into the water. Mubeccel asked what the fare would be to take us to Antalya and the conductor said there was no fare.

"You have paid enough with your disappointment."

Kindness like this happened often to Rose and me when we visited Turkey.

We took a taxi from the bus station to Antalya. I sat up front and chatted with our driver. He said that his main occupation was a carpenter, but he also drove a taxi so he and his family could get by.

We rolled along, talking among ourselves and with the taxi driver, enjoying the beautiful day. We looked out at fields of wheat and cotton and olive groves. Farmers also planted olive trees, spaced at regular intervals, in their wheat fields. The old tractors used for harvesting allowed passage around the olive trees. Also, landowners hired nomads to harvest crops by hand. We could see their tents set up near the fields. Women cut the wheat with sickles and the men pitch-forked the cut wheat onto trucks.

Suddenly the car shuddered and I felt the tell-tell vibration of a blown-out tire. We got out and stretched our legs while the driver worked on replacing the blown-out tire with his spare. After a few minutes we noticed that he was struggling manfully to undue the lug nuts. It looked like the driver was experiencing the same problem endured by myself and many other drivers. Whoever installed the tire used way too much power to tighten the lug nuts holding the tire onto the wheel. The salty sea air corroded the lug nuts, adding to the difficulty of loosening them.

Standing on the roadside, I looked across a plowed field and saw abandoned construction equipment and a large truck. Maybe I could find a long pipe that the driver could use for leverage. I keep a pipe in my car's trunk for just such a purpose. I saw a couple of pipes lying on the ground but they were too small so I decided to climb up into the bed of the truck.

Once inside the pile looked much bigger and loomed over me. I had to be careful moving around among discarded machine parts, appliances and scrapped metal. Rusted edges, broken glass, and jagged ends of metal rods and pipes threatened my clothes and skin. I saw a likely looking pipe sticking out from under the mess and began to wrestle it around. The pile moved. I decided to look elsewhere in the truck.

I gingerly climbed the junk hill, trying to see if there were any pipes that might work for a lever. After finding pipes that were too big, too small, too short, or too long I finally spied a suitable one and worked it out of the pile. I carried it back to our driver and showed him how to use the pipe with his tire iron to loosen lug nuts.

Mubeccel said I shouldn't have walked through the field because there might be vipers. I wasn't sure if she was joking or not because the subject of vipers sometimes came up in a joking vein. That dated from our earlier trip to Aphrodisias, site of an ancient city dedicated to the goddess Aphrodite. Signs posted at Aphrodisias said "Dikkat! Yilan!" which meant "Beware! Snake!". Thereafter, while Mubeccel, Rose and I walked around the ancient ruins we periodically would point to bushes and say, "Bak, Yilan!" which meant "Look, Snake!" Sometimes just to startle Rose and Mubeccel I would stiffen and yell, "Dikkat!" "Kus!" meaning, "Beware! Bird!"

Our driver strained at the lug nuts, the pipe set over an arm of the tire iron giving him four feet or so of added leverage. He heaved once, twice, and on his third mighty heave, bent the pipe.

I set off again towards the field and the abandoned truck. Mubeccel became alarmed and said to Rose, "You must control David. He might get bit by a viper."

I replied, "I didn't see any when I went the first time.

Besides, the day is too hot for snakes to be out."

Nevertheless, this time when I crossed the field I did watch for snakes. I did the same when I climbed again into the shaky pile of metal scraps. If I were superstitious, I might have imagined the pile of metal and glass resented being disturbed. The place was so quiet, no bird calls, no wind, just the ominous wreckage I needed to revisit. Some ancient ruins were said to be haunted, why not this place, some jinn of junk perhaps?

Parts of the mass moved and metal grated on metal as I worked out another pipe. The walls of this pipe were too thin, however, and would probably bend. I carefully climbed around some more. I knew that if I got pinned down by a metal avalanche it would be several minutes before Mubeccel and Rose figured out they should check on me. A slight injury would be bad and a serious injury could be disastrous. Mubeccel's remark about vipers added to my tension.

Ahh, there was a nice strong-looking pipe. I just needed to wiggle it a bit and...the pile began to slide towards me. I dodged and the slide paused, caught up by some other piece of junk. I waited a bit for things to settle down—including my heart rate—took a deep breath, and continued looking. I saw the pipe I had tried to pull free, but what looked like a metal cabinet rested against it now. I imagined it sliding forward and pinning me and decided not to push my luck with that particular pipe.

I looked around for several minutes more and found what I hoped would be a suitable pipe. I wrestled it out carefully and gingerly threaded my way through the mass. I took care to jump away from the truck when I descended, fearing I might disturb a snake napping in the shade under the truck.

I crossed the field again and as I approached our taxi I heard Mubeccel say to Rose,

"You must control David. He will get hurt."

"This should do the trick," I said and held up the pipe.

Our driver gratefully took the pipe from me and went to work. This pipe was stronger than the first one. Years of carpentry had made our driver strong and again he heaved. Another mighty heave broke the tire iron.

By this time Mubeccel determined she should call for help. Luckily, she had cell phone service out here in the countryside. Because we were outside the city limits the military police, or gendarmes, responded and arrived in about twenty minutes.

An olive-drab military van pulled up next to the taxi. Half a dozen gendarmes spilled out. All carried submachine guns except an officer who wore a pistol at his waist. Three gendarmes spread out and positioned themselves at the rear of the truck, holding their weapons at the ready. Mubeccel caught my startled reaction. "In case bad people come."

I realized that to criminals, stranded motorists might appear to be ripe fruit ready for the picking, although my years of travel in Turkey had only been positive. Turks have been unfailingly helpful and friendly wherever we went.

Three gendarmes not guarding the road took over heaving on the pipe with their better quality tire iron. The pipe bent. Leaving four gendarmes behind for protection, the officer and driver took off to find a mechanic. Thirty minutes later the van returned with a mechanic who attacked the tire iron with a hammer, but the lug nuts didn't budge. I wondered if the lug nuts would get rounded and have to be cut off with a torch. Maybe it was just as well that the gendarmes' tire iron broke before that happened.

The soldiers took off again and found a second mechanic. This man, older but heavily built and very fit-looking, might have been a blacksmith. He carried a serious-looking crescent wrench and a heavy hammer. Even so, it was hard going. I wanted to find another pipe, but this time I went along with the pleas of Rose and Mubeccel to "be safe."

The burly mechanic hammered for several minutes. Every lug nut had to be hammered loose. Finally the lug nuts were off, and our driver rolled the spare tire up and set it on the wheel. Mubeccel walked up behind the mechanic to thank him just as he straightened up from his efforts. He turned around, began to say something, then bent over and vomited. Our hero mechanic had exerted himself to the point of becoming sick.

Mubeccel helped us figure out what to pay the mechanic, and Rose and I knew enough Turkish to thank the gendarmes. I think they appreciated us being able to speak their language. We surely appreciated their help.

Rose and Mubeccel noticed my shirt was torn and stained with rust. A long but shallow scratch had left an impressive smear of blood on my stomach. I was so concentrated on getting a pipe and thinking about snakes that I hadn't noticed the torn shirt or the scratch. At least I hadn't torn my pants or got a nail through my canvas shoes, though I wore smudges of grime on my clothes and arms and even my face from wiping perspiration off my forehead.

Mubeccel shook her head.

"You should control David."

Chapter 3

SURPRISE PARTY IN BISHKEK

The bus carried Rose and me to Istanbul International Airport as the pre-dawn's light revealed scores of sheep tethered on hilltops. When the sun broke over the horizon the sheep would be slaughtered, throats cut, beginning Kurban Bayrum, (Sacrifice Holiday), to celebrate the end of the Ramadan fasting month. The festival event and our trip coincided with May 9, Victory Day for the Union of Soviet Socialist Republics, commemorating victory over Germany.

The Turkish Airlines flight to Kazakhstan's capitol, Alma Alta (Father of Apples) took about eight hours. For some reason Alma Alta has been renamed Almaty. I don't know what, if anything, the new name means. We clutched our bags and pushed through the crowd, sometimes being carried along by the mass of people lining up for customs. The terminal was packed and hot. We made our way through the press of people, through customs, and saw someone holding a sign that read, "Dr. Rose Marino University of Kansas. This was our ride to Bishkek, the capitol of Kyrgyzstan, where we were to stay for two weeks.

Once we got into the countryside we saw Kazak horsemen riding herd on cattle. Instead of cowboy hats the Kazaks wore canvas fedoras. I very much wanted to stop and try to buy one but the driver didn't understand my request. He spoke Russian, not English. We might have been able to communicate with him in Turkish but at that time we didn't know how similar Kyrgyz was to Turkish. Anyway, we had a four-hour ride ahead of us and the driver probably wanted to get that over with.

Our time in Kyrgyzstan was part of a scholar exchange program between Kyrgyzstan International University and the University of Kansas. Rose was to lecture on international law. I volunteered to be an English speaker for one or two English classes at the university.

We passed through foothills on which stood sculptures of heroic workers and soldiers. The sculpture I liked best, though, was that of a snow leopard. The figure must have been ten feet tall, for it was easily visible from the road. Our driver had seen it many times and so drove right on past. I didn't know what to say to the driver to get him to stop.

Respek Zirulbek, President of Kyrgyzstan International University, met Rose and I when we arrived in Bishkek. Respek first took us to our apartment, one in a series of high-rise apartments erected during the Gorbachev era. Respek carried Rose's luggage and would have carried mine also but I assured him I could do that.

Respek pushed the wrong number for our floor so our elevator stopped one floor below where we were to stay. The door opened and there in the foyer three Kyrgyz men were butchering a sheep and throwing the parts into a claw-footed bathtub. The men stared at us. We stared at them. The Kyrgyz men hadn't seen many Westerners and we had never seen men butchering a sheep in an elevator foyer. Respek pushed a button and the doors closed. "Country people," he said.

Seconds later we were stepping into our apartment where we dropped off our bags. Respek warned us not to open the door to any strangers, even if they claimed to be police. Respek explained that a visiting professor had opened his door to some men claiming to be police only to be robbed by them. They not only robbed him but took all of his clothes, even the ones he was wearing. They figured he would be too embarrassed to leave his apartment to go for help.

The real police caught the robbers, who turned out to be members of the Kyrgyz Olympic Boxing Team. They received nine-year prison sentences. Respek said they may not live that long. He didn't explain why he said that but I guessed it had something to do with embarrassing their country.

Respek drove us to the food bazaar where we were amazed at the bounty before us—rows of smoked chicken, walls of raw sheep and beef, bins of onions, cabbages, parsley, jugs of goat milk and tables of goat cheese filled the gymnasium-sized indoor bazaar. Respek noted our eyes open with surprise and wonder.

"We are not like the Chinese. We do not eat snakes and cockroaches."

We selected a variety of items, all purchased and carried by Respek. As we walked to the car, we passed a street vendor selling delicious-smelling meat pies. I had to have one and it tasted as delicious as it smelled. Rose tried to stop me because I had recently recovered from an intense digestive disorder but I suffered no ill effects from the street food.

I also tried Kumis, fermented mare's milk, which is a popular and potent alcoholic drink. Respek nodded approvingly and gestured towards a pickup truck on the bed of which sat a huge keg and next to the keg a board hung with dried fish.

"Kyrgyz Happy Hour. How about a Kyrgyz beer?"

I declined the dried fish but tried the beer, which reminded me of cut-rate American beer.

Respek delivered us with our groceries to our apartment and said that a woman named Raisa would soon stop by. Raisa, a liaison for the exchange program, visited just after we moved in. She ensured we were satisfied with our apartment, which was truly nice, and she invited us to a welcoming party.

"We will have it here." Raisa gestured around our spacious apartment. "You don't have to do anything. We will see you at 5:00."

Raisa left. Rose and I rested for awhile from our culture shock and jet lag and tiredness from ten hours of air travel to reach Almaty and four hours riding in the van to Bishkek. As I drifted off to sleep the images I had seen flitted across my closed eyes: Goats slaughtered on hills at dawn in Turkey; The goat butchered in an elevator foyer in Bishkek; Shopping the Food Bazaar; Drinking Kumis and beer; Invited to a party in our honor at our apartment. All we had to do was stay where we were.

We were to find out that such hospitality was the norm when we traveled in Central Asia. Bishkek and the faculty and staff and their spouses from Kyrgyz International University, descendants of Genghis Khan's Golden Horde, would be our friends and companions for the next two weeks.

Kyrgyzstan owns the proud tradition of the longest oral history, *The Epic of Manas*, the most treasured expression of the national heritage of the Kyrgyz people. *The Epic of Manas* has been related in oral form by various singers throughout the centuries. As nomads, the Kyrgyz had no written language. However, they excelled in oral composition, which they artistically employed in their traditional poetry and epic songs. Its longest version, consisting of half a million poetic lines, was written down from one of the last master-manaschï (singers of Manas) Saiakbai Karalaev (1894-1971). The epic is indeed unique in its size. It is twenty times longer than the Homeric epics Iliad (15693) and Odyssey (12110) taken together and two and a half times the length of the Indian epic Mahabharata.

Guests began arriving right at 5:00. Respek, Zirulbek, Raisa, and their spouses and friends and colleagues at Kyrgyz International University welcomed us. Somehow we all got seated at a very long table. I hadn't paid attention to it because our kitchen had a very nice breakfast nook that suited Rose and I very well.

Respek broke bread and passed pieces around the table. I recalled then that to "break bread" in our own past referred to dining. Breaking bread, we observed later, was always done by the head of the family or the highest ranking person at the dinner.

Before we began dining Respek filled everyone's small glass with cognac. Rose said she didn't drink cognac. Respek shrugged and moved to fill my glass. I said that I didn't drink cognac either. Conversation around the table stopped. Everyone stared at me. I recovered quickly and said that I would be happy to try their cognac. Frozen faces relaxed immediately into smiles.

First, Respek raised his glass in a welcoming toast for Rose and me. As the dinner progressed, each person at the table raised a glass and proposed a toast, sometimes to Rose and me, sometimes to Respek, sometimes to Manas, the King Arthur of Kyrgyzstan, and so on. Each toast meant knocking back one more shot glass of cognac. All of us cognac drinkers acquired rosy faces after a few glasses. Rose was allowed to make her toast with water. She greatly impressed our Kyrgyz friends by speaking Russian. Rose was to find that her memory of Russian increased a bit each day.

Russian was still the official language of Kyrgyzstan, just as it was for Kazakhstan and Uzbekistan, which we visited at the end of our Central Asian odyssey. We learned that the individual languages of the countries we visited were making a comeback. This helped our communication because both Kyrgyz and Uzbeks could understand our Turkish a bit. Kyrgyz regard Kyrgyzstan as the Mother Country of Turkey. Not only were we able to communicate with them but were able to do so in their mother tongue. I stumbled along as best I could but Rose, using some Russian and better Turkish than I got along very well.

When it came time for me to do my toast I said it in English, thanking everyone for their welcome and the wonderful dinner. And a wonderful dinner it was. The dinner included some wonderful dishes—monte (a kind of meat dumpling), a kind of stew using thick noodles, chicken, grilled lamb, sausages of some kind, not much in the way of vegetables. Cabbage was omnipresent, I believe, because it could withstand the harsh climate better than lettuce.

At some point in the evening one of the Kyrgyz turned to me and remarked, "You must be tired of cognac." I said that I probably had had enough cognac, whereupon my friend said, "Of course, how about some champagne?" So both Rose and I tried Kyrgyz champagne and it was very good.

Raisa and one or two Kyrgyz steered Rose and I away from the table into our living room and we talked while everyone else cleared the table and washed all the dishes. When everything was cleared, cleaned, and put away our hosts bid good night and we settled into our first night in Kyrgyzstan.

Chapter 4

DOWN INDEPENDENCE PASS

My college roommate, John Retrum, and I had become friends during my last semester of graduate school and his last semester as a graduating senior majoring in Biology at the University of Kansas. John invited me to come out to Aspen, Colorado, and visit him after we finished school that May. John had been raised in Aspen and was dismayed that Aspen had become a major tourist destination, but he assured me he knew some good hiking and camping spots.

So, with that in mind, after receiving a note from John reminding me of his invitation, I set off for Aspen in my ten-year-old '62 Oldsmobile Super 88. The big car devoured the Kansas highways, but when I got into Colorado and began to climb into the mountains, I found my '88 didn't have the pep it demonstrated in the rolling prairie of Kansas. This really became apparent as I approached Independence Pass, ninety-five miles outside of Denver and about twenty miles from Aspen.

My route, chosen for scenery rather than ease of driving, took me up Independence Pass. Part of State Highway 82, at 12,095 ft. it is the highest paved state highway over the Continental Divide in Colorado, in the Sawatch Range of the Rocky Mountains. Though it is a paved road, it can be narrow and winding and therefore difficult to traverse in poor weather. It also has steep drop offs in places along the route.

As I approached the highway leading up to Mt. Evans, I saw a hitchhiker standing by the road. I had hitchhiked some, so I picked up the college-aged young man. I mentioned I was headed for Aspen and he replied that was the general direction he was headed.

Construction near the summit halted the string of vehicles. I should have shut off my engine, but thought that we would only be idling a few minutes. The few minutes turned into several minutes and the old '88 overheated and the engine quit. When it came time to start up, the engine was too hot. I had lost some water from the radiator also. My hitchhiker friend took my water container and, after carefully removing the radiator cap added to the diminished supply. My engine was still too hot to start again, however, and cars had to pull around us to continue their way to the summit and down Independence Pass.

A few minutes later a Winnebago appeared and the driver offered to push my car. "You can start it once you get moving," he said. That made sense to me so I agreed to his offer.

Once over the summit I began to coast down. I found out right away that with no engine running I had neither power steering nor power brakes. The ease in turning provided by power steering became the reverse condition without the engine on. The grade became steeper and the curves became sharper. I pulled back on my steering wheel in order to push the brakes enough to slow down even as I struggled to turn the steering wheel. I tried to start the engine several times but had no luck doing that. I glanced at my hitchhiker companion and he looked tense. I imagine I looked tense too, because I sure felt tense.

I closed in on a truck that was having trouble of some sort. Smoke poured from its rear tires or maybe its brakes as the driver tried to slow down his vehicle. I pulled back on my steering wheel as hard as I could and pressed my foot into the brake as hard as I could, but I inexorably glided closer and closer to the truck, its smoke now drifting onto my windshield.

I stole a glance at my companion and his face was white as the snow we had seen by the road. I guess if I had been able to slow down enough, the hitchhiker might have leapt out, and I would have understood.

Finally, I had to ram the truck or pass it. I pulled back on the steering wheel and pressed my foot into the brake pedal even as I turned out to pass the truck. I was lucky no vehicles were coming toward me. I quickly turned back into the right lane just as an oncoming vehicle appeared. I hoped my heart wasn't pounding so hard it would make me pass out. I imagined it must be bruising the inside of my chest, and I guess my hitchhiker must be feeling about the same. A quick glance showed me his eyes wide and his face white. I assume we both must have been breathing but I didn't notice.

More turns, more braking, and at last we reached the bottom. The engine had cooled enough for me to start the engine. I pulled into the nearest turnoff, a service station. "I'll get off here," said my companion.

Can't say that I blamed him.

Chapter 5

10,000 ISLANDS; 10,000 PADDLE STROKES

A chain of islands and mangrove islets off the coast of southwest Florida make up the Ten Thousand Islands. Rising sea level covered shoreline in some places, leaving high spots as islands. Mangrove islets take root on oyster bars and in turn the mangroves provide thousands of roots to which cling barnacles and oysters. The islands and mangrove islets only number in the hundreds. The name Ten Thousand Islands allegedly came about when someone tasked with counting each island gave up in frustration, saying "There must be ten thousand of them." Chokoloskee Bay lies between Everglades City and the Ten Thousand Islands.

Son-in-law, Mike Randolph, had accompanied neighbor Tom Cottin and other friends on kayak trips to the Ten Thousand Islands several times and asked me if I would like to join them. This seemed like an ideal winter vacation so I readily agreed to come. The plan was to set out across mile-wide Chokoloskee Bay, at Everglades City, at 8:00 a.m. so as to miss the incoming tide and to avoid the wind, sure to rise as the day progressed. Our kayak provider didn't get them to us until about 10:00 a.m. By that time the tide was coming in strongly and the wind had risen from the expected 5 knots to 20 knots or so. Wind-whipped whitecaps speckled the mile-wide bay. A storm farther west began to come through our area driving clouds that soon became a grey overcast on Chokoloskee Bay. A Park Ranger had advised against going but our leader, Tom, was not to be deterred.

Had I been faced with such wind on little Lone Star Lake in Kansas I would not have put a boat in. Nevertheless our leader decided we should go. The idea was that once we got into the mangroves they would shelter us from the wind. This was no leisurely paddle. I had to dig in and paddle hard each stroke. I remembered how Rose had been concerned that the exertion from shoveling snow would bring on a heart attack. This effort here was way beyond any exertion caused by shoveling snow, when I could stop anytime. Stopping to rest here meant being carried backward by the tide and wind. Stopping also meant a greater chance of being turned broadside and swamped by the wind-driven waves. Twice I had "crabbed" my paddle, which meant I had dug my paddle in on the windward side just as a wave struck the paddle. The effect was as if an unseen hand had grasped my paddle and tried to use it to pull me over.

Waves broke continually over my kayak and spilled into the cockpit. I had dislodged my skirt after hitting it with my knee while feeling for the left rudder pedal. The skirt was to hug my waist and fit snugly around the cockpit, thus preventing water, at least not much water, from spilling into the boat. I was paddling as hard as I could and we had just begun our passage. It was horrible, and exhausting. Several times I thought I was going to be swamped and drowned.

Mike and I reached a tide marker about halfway across the bay. We grasped the tide marker and planned our course. Our destination, Tiger Key, lay to the south and east, directly into the face of the wind. Mike consulted his map. We each carried a waterproof map lashed to the boat right in front for easy access. Mike suggested that we try to avoid the wind by heading around the mangroves that bordered the south side of Chokoloskee Bay. Once around, Mike reasoned, we would hug the edge of the mangroves and using the map to guide us, thread our way to Tiger Key. Mike yelled to Tom and Joe about our plans to try to avoid paddling directly into the wind. Tom and Joe decided to take the most direct route, but that route meant they would paddle directly into the wind. I was not that strong a paddler. Our passage across the bay should have taken thirty minutes but it took us ninety minutes, sixty minutes more of paddling than expected, hard paddling at that.

I finally made my way around the mangrove islands, turned south and encountered big rolling waves, perhaps four feet high, higher than my head anyway. I knew I could not make my way through them, which is what I told Mike. He is a good son-in-law. He didn't abandon me to my fate.

We became lost working our way through the mangroves and the tide narrowed and became stronger, but we had no choice other than to paddle against the current. We found a chickasee, a Calusa Indian word for a platform built out from land, and beached our boats and rested an hour while we waited for the tide to slack. We still felt we could make our way to Tiger Key and after the tide lessened quite a bit we set off. Mike had consulted my Garmin (Global Position Locator or GPS) and thought he could figure out a route through the maze of mangroves. Problem was there were mangroves too small for the Garmin to pick up but big enough to obscure our vision. Also, sitting in the kayaks meant our heads were only three feet above the water's surface, too low for an advantageous viewing position.

We decided to return to the chickasee, but we could not

find it after turning back from the ocean rollers. We had been out six hours or so and we were lost. Despite their name, mangrove islands are not islands in the sense that one may beach a boat and step out onto land. There is no beach and there is no land, only thick fingers of mangrove roots reaching into the water, covered with razor-sharp oysters and barnacles. No place to camp. What looked like beach from a distance proved to be oyster beds that the rising tide would cover in a few hours. Also, the rudder on Mike's kayak quit working. This meant that when confronted by adverse winds we had to lash our kayaks together so I could use my rudder to direct our progress.

We had about 40 minutes of daylight left when the setting sun fell on an eight-foot high bluff to which we paddled, climbed, and chose for our campsite. I set up my tent while Mike unloaded what we needed from our kayaks. Brush and trees left just enough room to erect the tent though I had to yield to a tree so the normal square shape of the tent became more like a K. Still, it was really good to have shelter and not spend the night shivering and wet in our kayaks. Tent up and bedding taken care of we set up our camping chairs and caught our breath. I think we turned in about 7:30. Mike said he slept pretty well but I did not, although I was warm enough and should have been tired enough to drop off.

Next morning we waited for the tide to slack before setting out. We carefully checked over our camping area to make sure we weren't leaving any litter. The only sign anyone had been there might have been deduced from bent brush. I did lose one tent stake in the underbrush. I suppose a swamp ape could find the tent stake and use it as a toothpick. We had several miles to go just to return to our departure point. I was too exhausted to endure another bay crossing and Mike agreed with my suggestion that we ask for a rescue. We found a low tide oyster bed to beach our kayaks and set up our chairs while we consulted the map and my Garmin. We had to be very careful not to lose our balance on the uneven oyster bed and fall to be cut up by the sharp shells. I was able to use my Garmin to establish our coordinates which Mike gave to the dispatcher after calling 911. Because Mike told the dispatcher that his partner, me, was seventy years old, the Park Service was concerned about my health.

About an hour after Mike's call a Park Ranger boat arrived to rescue us (me really because Mike could have gone on alone). The first question they asked was if we had any injuries or other health concerns. Probably in my case they were concerned about a heart attack or a stroke. The Park Ranger said the service rescued 65 people a year in this area. Once ashore we carried the kayaks back to where we had begun, loaded our rental car and drove back to Ivey House. There, we got a room for the night and unloaded our gear, emptying our dry bags of everything so we could see what needed to be washed and what could be thrown away.

Mike hauled laundry items in to the Ivey House washroom and I sorted through my things. As I was doing this as a young woman came up and asked if I was getting ready to go. I related to her my experience, which I believe she found a bit unsettling because this was to be her first time. She was joined by another young woman and we talked a bit. I emphasized the importance of using the skirt to help keep water out of the boat. Neither had heard about that and I wondered what their experience would be. I hoped they would have a better time than I did and wished them luck.

Back home, checking Wikipedia for basic information on the Ten Thousand Islands I found this statement. "Since this is a wilderness area where wind, weather and lack of fresh water can become threatening, the Wildlife Service recommends only seasoned canoeists and sea kayakers attempt the trip."

I don't plan on doing this again, ever.

Chapter 6

A VISIT TO THE EIFFEL TOWER

Rose and I decided that we should visit the Eiffel Tower before we left Paris for Normandy. This was the 100th anniversary of its construction even though the "Tour Eiffel" was originally meant to be temporary when built to celebrate the centenary of the French Revolution. We arrived in the early evening just after sunset and the tower was lit up. We were puzzled to see the Eiffel Tower cordoned off with ribbon and car barriers. "Was the tower under repair?" I asked a bystander.

My informant explained that the area was secured because former President Reagan would visit the Eiffel Tower tomorrow as part of France's bicentennial. Rose and I were both taken aback by this, disappointed and upset that our wish to see the Eiffel Tower could not be fulfilled. We reasoned that Reagan could travel to France and see the Eiffel Tower anytime he wanted, and at our expense. We, on the other hand, had traveled to France on our hard-earned money only to be thwarted because of politics.

We decided to sit for awhile and think over the situation. Rose sipped her wine and I my beer. From our outside table we could see the great tower's immense base and also could make out portions of the structure through the trees.

"Let's at least walk around the outside," said Rose.

"Right," I said. "Let's just walk around the outside."

I think at that moment we both knew what we were going to do although neither one of us voiced the idea. Rose and I began to survey the scene. Police and security people stood around, looking bored. After all, Reagan wouldn't arrive until the next day.

We strolled slowly around the barriers, noting where security and police loitered. We spotted several gaps in the barriers and noted those also. We made special note of those gaps where security staff were absent.

We stepped back occasionally and looked up and up, unable to see the top from this close vantage point. Vendors sold Eiffel Tower T-shirts, Eiffel Tower pencil sharpeners, color slides of the Eiffel Tower bathed in colored floodlights, and other knick-knacks celebrating the engineering triumph of Alexandre Gustave Eiffel.

We made a complete circuit of the Tower and came to one of the gaps where no security staff was present.

"The hell with Reagan," I said. "Let's go in."

Rose said, "Right! Let's go."

We stepped past an unwatched barrier. Once past, we walked quickly as though we belonged there. We gambled that if we walked openly, someone might think we were part of the security or publicity detail and leave us alone.

We wanted to get off the ground floor as quickly as possible, so we made our way to the elevator. I pressed the UP button. Nothing happened. We heard no rumble of a descending car. "Let's find the stairs," I suggested. We turned away from the elevator just as several men ran up, plain clothes security I guess.

We feigned innocence, which, while not convincing the security detail that we belonged, perhaps influenced them to simply point to the exit rather than arrest us. We walked out,.

Chapter 7

ELMIRA AND THE BUFFALO

A drizzling mist drifted with us as we drove west from Lawrence along Kansas Interstate 70, that November. Three women, Elmira and Gulnara from Kyrgyzstan and Yumi from Japan, and a young man, Rustam, also from Kyrgyzstan, accompanied me. The Kyrgyz were economics scholars who had come to the University of Kansas in an exchange program with Bishkek Technological University in Bishkek, Kyrgyzstan. Yumi, a graduate student from Japan, had met them in an economics class at the university. All of them wanted to see the American buffalo.

Rustam looked out at the November mist-shrouded morning.

"This is a poet's kind of day."

Yumi said, "Yes, a Japanese poet would get much material from our drive today."

My Kyrgyz friends and Yumi would return to their homes in a couple of weeks and wanted to see more of Kansas before they left. Being a devotee of Kansas history and its flora and fauna, I had asked them if they would like to take a day trip with me to see some sights, including buffalo. They readily agreed.

Elmira said, "We think the buffalo may be similar to our yak." Elmira pronounced buffalo as "boofulo."

"Soon, we will be able to see for ourselves," said Gulnara.

"This is exciting!" said Rustam. "Thank you for taking the time to do this."

"Rose and I were treated so well when we visited Kyrgyzstan and Uzbekistan that this is just a small gesture on my part."

We drove in silence through the mist and rolling land of the Smoky Hills in central Kansas.

"Much of this land was under an inland sea 100 million years ago," I said. "People can find fossils of ocean life right here in Kansas, the middle of the United States."

"I can imagine the rolling hills as ocean waves frozen in time," said Rustam.

"You do have a poet's eye," said Gulnara.

The overcast increased and by the time we reached Longford, in Clay County, the sky promised rain. Still, I was not going to end our trip without showing my friends some buffalo, up close if possible. I had seen buffalo up very close several years before, when I walked through Ray Smith's buffalo herd. I was on a bus trip with friends and I thought it would be entertaining to have a film shot of the bus we rode in, driving through the herd up to the hill where Ray Smith had built a 15'x17' cement sculpture of a buffalo. I heard a few years after that Ray had been trampled by his own buffalo, not in a stampede, but just as the buffalo ambled to another pasture and brushed him aside, maybe not even noticing he was there. The buffalo gave him a broken collarbone and broken leg. That first time, as I walked up the path through the herd I could hear their heavy breathing and smell their strong but not unpleasant animal scent. I had no idea what danger I was in. I don't know why Ray hadn't stopped me from walking through the herd. Maybe he was too shocked at the notion that anyone would do something so reckless. I didn't intend to get so close to the buffalo on this visit, nor allow my friends to do so, either.

The Coachlight Restaurant in Longford has so many people stop there to ask directions to Ray Smith's buffalo ranch that they have directions printed for visitors. Several Longford residents were at supper in the restaurant and they were very curious and friendly towards these visitors. I said that Yumi was from Japan and that the other visitors were from Kyrgyzstan, on the other side of the earth from Kansas. I explained that if they had a globe and put a finger on Kansas, and kept the same latitude and slid the finger to the other side of the globe the finger would rest on Kyrgyzstan.

"We want to see the boofulo," said Elmira, the others nodding vigorously.

"Well," said one restaurant regular, "he's got 'em, but you better get out there before it rains. Those dirt roads can be nasty to drive on once they turn to mud."

"Gonna get dark soon, too," cautioned another. "Easy to get lost if you don't follow the directions."

I knew this because I had failed to find Ray Smith's ranch on another visit, coming from the west, even though I had been to the ranch a few times before. We finished our meal and with the well wishes of the Coachlight customers and staff set off for the buffalo ranch. The directions were flawless.

It was dark when I pulled into the ranch house yard. I guessed it would be too late for my friends to see the buffalo, but I thought it would be impolite not to let Ray know who was pulling into his driveway. Besides, I wanted to give him a copy of Sampling Kansas, my book about little-known places and events in Kansas, in which I featured Ray Smith in my story about near-extermination of buffalo in Kansas and his efforts to build a herd.

Ray ran a finger around his globe from Kansas to the other side, where it came to rest on Kyrgyzstan.

"Other side of the earth, huh? I'll show them some buffalo. I'll guide you up a little hill in my truck. That's where the buffalo will be about now. If you get stuck I can pull you out all right."

Ray and I stepped outside to the shouts of my friends.

"A lynx, a lynx! It tried to get in my window." Elmira had rolled her window down before I shut off the engine and left the car. Without power the electric window would not close.

"I used Rustam's umbrella to block him from climbing in the window. He almost got me."

The rest of my friends were pretty excited too.

Ray laughed. "Oh, that was only Patches. He's a cougar cub, not a lynx. Patches has the run of the place."

In addition to raising buffalo, Ray Smith kept lions, tigers, and bears— animals that people had bought or somehow got possession of but couldn't handle as they got bigger. I had seen the animals before and Ray would have taken us to see them now if it weren't so late.

Ray looked around for Patches but he was nowhere to be seen.

"Patches likes to ride with me in the cab of my truck. He probably thought he could ride with you and your friends. You must have scared him off."

Rustam volunteered to ride with Ray. The rest of us followed in my car, through tall grass and up a hill. We reached the hilltop just as rain began to fall. Out on that hilltop, miles from any town, it was pitch black. Ray's truck was not very far away but I could barely see it except when lightning flashed.

Lightning lit up the sky and hooves shook the ground as scores of buffalo galloped by my car. One buffalo stopped on the driver's side of my car, lowered his head and peered in. We were eyeball to eyeball, his head much too big to fit in the window if I had foolishly opened it. His curly pelt and curved horns glistened with rain. He loped off and more buffalo continued to gallop past the car. The interior dome light clicked on. To my horror I saw Elmira open her door and step out.

"Elmira, get back in the car!"

With the door open I could hear the heavy breathing of the buffalo as they ran past us. Small flashes from Elmira's camera and larger lightning flashes illuminated Elmira aiming her camera at dark, massive shapes hurtling past her. I yelled repeatedly to Elmira, joined by the pleas of Gulnara and Yumi, to get back in the car. Finally, Elmira got back inside.

"Elmira, you could have been trampled and killed out there. I was afraid for you."

"Me too," said Elmira. "I was scared." I hoped she had gotten some good photos.

I blinked my lights to let Ray know we were ready to move on. We followed him to a trailer he had set up as a souvenir gallery. From reading newspaper articles about Ray and my past conversations with him I knew Ray had traveled quite a bit. Ray liked to gather rocks from places he visited, and his collection included a stone from the Great Wall of China. He displayed memorabilia of these trips on shelves and behind glass cases.

Suddenly the trailer door banged open.

"The lynx, the lynx!" My friends pressed themselves into the farthest corner of the trailer.

Ray grinned. "Why, Patches. Where have you been?"

Patches walked in like he owned the place. He was about the size of a bobcat or lynx. His beautiful tan and gold and pinkish hide shown wet. I knelt down on the floor while my friends were shouting, "No, no," and Patches trotted right up to me.

I stroked his back and saw that he was very wet and heard him purring. Patches rubbed his rough muzzle against my face. I noticed right away that Patches' head was just slightly smaller than my own, and when he rubbed my face his lips curled back, revealing large, sharp teeth. I stood up.

Patches saw the other strangers pressed into the corner and headed over towards them. The women screamed. Ray hustled Patches out the door and latched it so he couldn't come back in. We talked with Ray a bit longer, him asking the Kyrgyz questions about Kyrgyzstan and its people and animals. They told Ray about yaks and snow leopards and other animals. I told Ray that while in Kyrgyzstan I had seen a large sculpture of a snow leopard set along a mountainside highway. I explained to my friends that Ray had erected a large sculpture of a buffalo on a hill on his ranch, but it was too dark to see now.

We bid our goodbyes and Ray walked with us to the car. Gulnara opened the door. Patches charged out of the darkness and jumped right into the back seat. He sat there clearly expecting a ride and possibly wondering about the excited antics of the visitors. Patches refused to budge, so Ray slid into the back seat and pushed him out. "Not this time, Patches."

We again bid goodbye and thanks to Ray, and Patches, and began our drive back to Lawrence. My friends talked about their day for awhile and fell asleep. I drove on to Lawrence, grateful for the good time had by the Kyrgyz and Yumi, thankful that some hand of Providence had protected Elmira from being trampled by the buffalo, and smiling at the thought of Patches, purring, his rough muzzle rubbing my face.

PART II -
STORIES TOLD TO ME

Chapter 8

ADVENTURES ON THE RAILS

By John Fuller as told to David Hann

Your Uncle Earl and I hopped freights in my first experience riding the rails. Later on, I and friends Dolby and Kidder decided to go up to the Dakotas and follow the harvest after we finished helping with the harvesting at home. We were all in our twenties then. World War I had come and gone. I had been trained as a medic, but the war ended and I was discharged before going anywhere outside of Tacoma, where I was stationed at Camp Lewis.

So we finished harvesting after a few days and went to Goodland and caught the main line on the railroad, a through freight. We had no suitcases, just handkerchiefs to carry some belongings and the clothes we had on. We found a hill where we could see a train coming a long way off and where the train would be slowed down by pulling up the hill. After checking to see that no railroad bulls were riding topside to spot us hoboes, we broke out from our hiding place and run up to the train.

It was a long train and we had no trouble running along and swinging aboard. You have to swing up on the space between the cars, then skin up the ladder and peek over the top, both ways. If the coast is clear you just climb on up. So we's on top and we each got a belt about sixty inches long. No, I wasn't that fat. I wore a regular belt too. We used the sixty-inch belts for something else. We'd unbuckle it after we got on top of the boxcar. The boxcar had about three one-by-fours running along the top. We fed one end of the buckle through the crack between the boards, brought it up, and buckled it around our middle. That way, if we went to sleep we wouldn't fall off, see?

We always had a breeze up there on the cars. We might catch rain sometimes and during midday the sun would've burnt us sure but we wore long sleeve shirts and of course we wore hats. If it rained or got cold we threw on our jackets or tried to find a car we could slip into. That was chancy.

Anytime you move around on a running train you might get thrown off by a sudden jerk or roll of the car on uneven track. Or you might slip into a boxcar where the current occupants don't want any company. Most times though us riders were pretty congenial and helped one another.

So we was riding along up top there, west of Norton a ways. We seen three guys on the boxcar ahead of us. Then we seen one of those guys slide off. We thought, "Oh, oh, he went to sleep." One of the guys peeled right off but the other turned and looked at us. Boy did he ever have a mean look. He stared right at me, like he was memorizing my face. Then he peeled off too.

We went on up towards Philipsburg and stopped for water on the way. A railroad workers strike was on and all the railroad guys was helping us. One of them warned us about what he called rough customers.

"Police are looking for a couple fellers, stabbed a guy just outside of Goodland, right on the train you rode. Threw him off the train and robbed him."

Well the last thing we wanted to do was to get mixed

up with the police, especially in a murder case so we didn't say anything about what we saw. We told the railroad guy that we'd be careful. The railroad guy said, "It looks rainy. Why don't you boys go up and get in one of those boxcars up there? There's one that has a load of coal. No reason you boys can't go up there and join 'em."

We went on up there and crawled in. The train pulled into Philipsburg and one guy in the boxcar was snoring. Good lord, he was snoring away, sleeping on these big lumps of coal. There was two cops down at the depot and they heard that guy snoring. The two cops got everyone of us out of there, lined us up and shook down every one of us. They told us,

"Boys, you might as well start walking. You'll never get out of here on a train."

I looked around at the bunch of us. That's when I seen the two guys who'd killed that man outside of Goodland.

"Hey, officer," I yelled. "We seen those two kill a man outside of Goodland." The two men took off running between the cars and the cops took out after them. The rest of us took off running too, in the opposite direction. The last thing we needed was to be held by the police as witnesses.

So, next morning early we went and got ourselves something to eat at a café. We talked with a little Greek, Nikos his name was, in the café. He'd been there for two weeks trying to get out. Nikos had been a coal miner around Fort Scott but there had been some anti-Greek trouble there so he lit out for a friendlier place.

"I got a girl back on Tinos that I'm going to send for and marry as soon as I can get some kind of regular job." Nikos explained that Tinos was an island just south of Athens. Dolby and Kidder and I wished him luck. We were all in the same fix pretty much, except that us three had a home to come back to. Of course we couldn't go back home with no money in our pockets and be a burden to our folks.

Nikos walked with us awhile 'till we got outside of town where we could hide and wait for a train. Nikos said, "I'm going to get out of here today or know the reason why." He cut down some alleys and we lost sight of him.

So we ambled outside of town and waited, hid in bushes, watching them make up a big freight train. We didn't see Nikos but figured he was hiding out nearby. The way they was making up the train with a lot of cars we knew they couldn't get up speed going up the grade right out of town. We could catch it easy because it was a long train that was going to start out slow.

Then a bobtail come out of the yard. That was an engine pulling about four boxcars and they was really barreling. We seen two guys try to catch it. I was close enough to them to see that they was the two killers and I guess they figured on catching a fast train. One of 'em couldn't run fast enough. The other guy caught it but he wished he hadn't. We heard him smack when he hit the side of the boxcar. Boy, did he roll when he hit the ground. It didn't kill him, but it sure did mess him up. We hoped the cops would find them but there weren't no cops riding the bobtail. The other guy scrambled into some bushes near the track.

Then came the big train but two cops was on top riding it out of town. They were determined to keep everybody off the train. We hid there watching the train come up the grade and cursing the cops. Then Nikos busted out of some bushes and he shot at those guys!

The cops shot back at him. He shot at them again, then he took off and the two cops peeled off the car and chased after him. They all three ran over a hill. Then it was like the Day of Judgment but instead of people rising from the grave there must have been a hundred guys who all rose from bushes around the track. We rushed for the train and made it. Nikos made it too! He circled around and grabbed one of the last boxcars.

Well our train rolled along all right but in the afternoon we ran into one of those real toad-strangler rains. Dolby said he'd noticed that a car with an open door had passed us when we hopped on, so we headed for that. We hurried along the top of the cars crouching down like monkeys, ready to grab for those slats because the rain mixed with the ashes from the coal-burning boiler made things slippery.

We swung down into the car and it wasn't very crowded. We seen several guys peel off the cars when the rain begun but we weren't about to get off lest we had to. We settled against a wall. There was some coal chunks lying around so all's we had to do was move 'em around a little so we could lie down, comfortable like, see?

It was during this period, the early 20s, that the expression "Hijack" originated. Guys would be in there, in a boxcar, and some guy would swing down from the top of the car into the door, and say, "Hi, Jack." Then he'd pull a gun and say, "Hi, Jack."

Well, that's what happened to us, only the fellow what swung down into the car and pulled a pistol was that killer we seen outside of Norton. He'd just come out of the light so his eyes wasn't adjusted to see inside the dark of the car. He just waved the pistol and said, "I want a little something from each one of you boys and no one will get shot."

Some of the men in the car began to fumble in their pockets but Dolby and Kidder and I knew that if the hijacker's eyes got used to the dark he might recognize us and shoot us. We looked at one another, grabbed a baseball-size hunk of coal each and let him have it. Now, Dolby was the pitcher for our Hill City ball team and me and Kidder played ball when we had the chance. We could all throw pretty hard and true and the killer never saw it coming.

Three chunks of coal hit the guy, two in the face and one in his chest by the neck. He let go of his handhold on the car and fell out backwards off the car. I don't know whether he got hurt or killed by falling off or not but we never saw him again

We rode on to just before the next stop, and peeled off the train just as it was slowing before entering the town. There was a long curve and the train slowed down enough for us to slide on off. Nikos joined us.

We made it to Omaha and one of the boys that was riding with us said, "Don't go down very far. The bulls are always looking around close to the rail yard."

So we dropped off just at the edge of the yard. We was walking along down there looking for a road that led to town and along came the biggest popeyed bulldog you ever hope to lay eyes on. He come and he wasn't saying nothing, but he was picking up his paws and putting them down. Well we took off running but the bulldog was gaining on us. We spied a pool of water and dashed right into it thinking that the bulldog wouldn't plunge into the water after us. He didn't but not because he didn't like water. He could smell what at first we didn't. Evidently a sewer had backed up and did that water stink. We went on through but the bulldog stopped at the edge of the water and stood there looking at us. Maybe I was imagining it but that bulldog looked like he was laughing.

We got to a lumberyard that had a old well there. We pumped water for each other and got cleaned up. We worked in Omaha for a street construction guy for three days and then hopped a freight on over to Council Bluffs. And you never saw so many bums in your life. They was all coming back and we was going the other way so the bulls didn't bother us. We hopped a freight and got up to Devil's

Lake, North Dakota.

We got to a ranch out there in the Dakotas and set to work with the harvesting. One of my jobs was driving a team of mules. I always treated the mules pretty well, grabbing a bit of grass for them as a treat and so forth, which might explain how I got lucky. About lunchtime I had a load on and didn't want to drive the whole thing in so I unhooked my mules, hopped on one mule and rode him in. When I got to the barn the old boy whose ranch it was stood there with his mouth wide open. "My god!" he said. "Kid, there's nobody's ever rode that mule before. He like to of killed the onlyest one that tried. And that harness there could've got you tore up pretty bad." Well I didn't try riding that mule again.

When that job played out we went on over across the Canadian line. They caught us over there and chucked us back across the border so we went a little further down the line and crossed over into Canada again. I forget the name of the town. We carried our belongings in a handkerchief, that's about all, and the clothes we had on. That's about all we had, no suitcase or nothing, that's all we had, see.

There was three weeks we didn't sleep in a bed. We slept in boxcars, courthouse steps, wherever, and we ate in the jungle with the rest of 'em. We'd buy a little meat to throw in the pot and everybody else did the same. Us hoboes were generally pretty good about sharing things and helping out them that needed it. Nobody shirked though. Nothing worse than being froze out of a small group of your fellow outcasts. And stealing? Maybe a pie cooling on a window sill or eggs from a hen house, maybe even a chicken, but nothing big or expensive. Nobody wanted to be the one what brought the cops down on us and stealing from boys in the jungle could get a person hurt pretty quick.

Well what some boys didn't realize was that with so

many of us looking for work you needed some kind of edge, some kind of advantage. One thing I learned from your Uncle Earl when I first rode the rails with him was to keep a clean pair of pants and a clean shirt rolled up in your kit. Riding the rails was dirty work and the work we did was hard and dirty too. Oh people knew that and made allowances but if you had to choose between hiring some shaggy and unshaved fellow in dirty clothes and somebody who looked somewhat civilized, who would you hire?

So I got into my clean clothes and went into a barber shop and found out a haircut and hot water shave would cost me fifty cents. Fifty cents! Why that would have took all my money and I was going to need a good breakfast if I got hired for labor work. I stood there considering and the barber says, "Tell you what, if I don't have to use my hot water I can get you spruced up for just 35 cents." Well I wasn't going to get a better deal so I told the old boy to go ahead. I got a haircut and a cold water shave that took all of 15 minutes. It cost me 35 cents and oh brother, was that cold water shave rough; but my fresh haircut and shave made me presentable enough to get a job. And the fifteen cents was enough for eggs, hash browns, and coffee.

Dolby and Kidder took off to try their luck in Idaho. Another kid, Bill Fabers and I got hired to help with the wheat harvest. The man we worked for called his horses his slaves. He says, "Now, Bill, you take care of the slaves. John, you do the stucking." That's the word they used for shocking the sheaves up there in Canada.

We went to bed that night and Bill says, "Man, I feel something biting me." I said, "So do I." We lit the lantern and you never seen so many bedbugs in your life. We picked them up and dropped them down the lamp chimney. They got to frying, so we quit. The next night, the lamp was clean, but it was the same process again. We stood it three nights. There was just as many the next night as there was the night before.

Bill came in the next morning and said, "Boy, we're having hot biscuits for breakfast this morning. I seen the old lady put 'em in the oven. "

We were sure excited at having hot biscuits, and we got to talking about our home-cooked meals and that made us more excited about the biscuits. We set down to the workers' table that sat outside our little bunkhouse, our mouths just watering for the biscuits. Well all we got was coffee, a bit of sidemeat, a couple of eggs and some slabs of mush.

We never saw any biscuits. The old lady only gave them to her husband. So we quit. Having to fight bedbugs every night was unpleasant and not getting biscuits was the last straw. We caught a freight that took us down to Jasper, Wyoming. Bill decided he would go up to South Dakota and see his sister so I was left on my own.

There was an old feller there in Jasper by the name of John White. We'd worked for him before. I looked him up and we talked a bit about my Canadian adventure and the bedbugs and no biscuits. He asked me what I intended to do. I said I guessed I would hop a freight to take me to Ansburough and try to get some kind of work there.

Mr. White said he wished I'd help him stack the last bit of wheat he had out there at his place. I says, "All right, but I'm afraid I'll get caught in the snow and that'd be a cold ride back sitting in a freight car."

Mr. White said, "Okay, the first snowflake that falls I'll take you into town." We worked out there three days and just had a small load left. A little old cloud about the size of your hat come over and it snowed like hell for about thirty seconds. Then the sun come out.

We got the load stacked and Mr. White took the reins and headed toward town. I said, "Where are you going?"

Mr. White said, "You kept your word and I'm gonna keep mine. So he took me to town and I caught a freight on in to Devil's Lake. Boy, it turned cold that night. I thought, it's sure going to be cold riding that freight tonight down to Ansburough.

I was sitting on a park bench near the railroad tracks trying to make up my mind where I wanted to go. An old boy come down and sat beside me and says, "Son, how far are you going?" Well in those days it weren't difficult to spot old boys who rode the rails so he had sized me up pretty well. I said, "Down to Kansas eventually." He says, "Can you drive a truck?" Well what farm boy doesn't know how to drive a truck so I says, "Well, sure." And he says, "How would you like to help me drive to Mesa City, Iowa? We won't stop. We'll just keep driving to Mesa City. There's a bed in the back of the truck and we'll take turns sleeping."

I says, "Okay." We drove on to Mesa City. We got there and unloaded the truck. I was standing there on the corner and damn if a truck didn't come by and driving it was a guy I knew. He said, "We'll go out together and see the town tonight."

We made the mistake of turning into an alley and two big shines walked up and showed us their pistols. I don't know what caliber the pistols were but the barrels looked like the end of a garden hose. When they got through with me and him all I had was eight Canadian nickels I had in a Bull Durham sack. My friend didn't have anything left. So we went up to our room and my friend looked around and found sixty cents and he gave that to me. He was going to get paid next day for delivering stuff in the truck but I thought that was still pretty generous.

I caught a freight train out next morning. Got to Deep River, Iowa, and they kicked me off. Now, Deep River was just a store and two or three buildings in the whole town.

I was sitting on the porch of the store when a guy come up there in a pickup truck. He come over and sat down beside me and says, "Where you headed?" I said, "I was headed for Kansas but they kicked me off the train." He says, "Well, how would you like to shuck some corn? Did you ever shuck corn?" I said, "Yeah, most I ever done was around sixty bushels." He says, "Well, I can't shuck either, but come on out and help me and two of us might make one hand." I says, "Okay" because I was broke.

I went out there and I was there shucking for oh, two weeks. If you ever shucked corn, you know you got to develop some calluses pretty quick or your hands will get rubbed raw. Well lucky for me I had done plenty of work that callused my hands but the fellow I joined up with his hands got to be pretty raw. He only worked there for two days and then he said, "You're doing all right." and he up and quit.

Now the way we shucked was to pull off the ears of corn and fling them against a sideboard where the corn ears bounced into the wagon pulled by a old slow-moving mule. I was shucking sixty bushels a day and the old boy in the field next to me was shucking 125 bushels a day. Bam, bam, bam, bam, bam, his ears of corn hit the sideboard like a hail storm." Sometimes the mule looked over his shoulder at me as if to ask, "Are you going to take all day?"

When we got through shucking the owner come up to me and he says, "John, how are you going to Kansas?" I said, "I'll grab a freight train." And he says, "The hell you are. You're going to ride. You aren't going to catch no freight train because it's too cold." The old boy goes down and he buys me a ticket to Norton, Kansas. I had around sixty dollars on me, too, see. That was pretty good money in those days.

I don't remember who it was, but I run across somebody from Hill City in Norton and I got a ride home. Our farm was near Penoke just west of Hill City. Nothing's there now but a grain elevator and post office mailbox. That was the end of that trip, and that was all the boxcar riding I wanted to do.

Chapter 9

BONNIE, IRENE & THE JACKRABBIT MAN

My Aunt Bonnie told me about letting the pigs out, and my mother, Irene told me about their adventure on the railroad bridge. I added the part about the Jackrabbit Man.

Louise Morgan regarded her two daughters, Irene and Bonnie. School was out for the summer and Louise thought about what chore she could assign them that would keep the girls out from underfoot and out of trouble. Their father Ray had asked Louise to make sure the girls, especially Bonnie, kept away from the pigs. "I swear, I don't know what gets into Bonnie, how she comes up with so many ways to cause a commotion."

"Swearing is what got into her," said Louise. "Bonnie was up in the loft watching you and the men round up the pigs. She admired everyone's swearing so much she wanted to hear it again."

After the men herded the pigs back into their pen and went in for lunch, Bonnie let the pigs out so she could hear the swear words again when the men re-penned the pigs. That cost her a switching, but none of the adults thought that experience would deter the mischievous eight-year-old for very long.

Louise said, "You girls go out and gather berries and we'll have shortcake and berries after supper tonight."

"What about the Jackrabbit Man?" asked Bonnie. The Jackrabbit Man, one Ernest Mulloy, or Jackrabbit Mulloy, had sworn vengeance on the Graham County sheriff, Brian Hopkins, for his role in capturing the notorious, though largely unsuccessful, bank robber and general bad man. Mulloy had escaped from the Hutchinson Correctional Facility several days before and rumors abounded as to his whereabouts.

"Oh, pooh on the Jackrabbit Man," said Louise, "If he has any sense he won't come near Graham County. He's probably headed up to Canada or Mexico or New York. There's plenty of criminals in New York he can associate with. You girls get out into the fresh air, and don't you dare go anywhere near that pig pen."

Bonnie and Irene stepped out into the morning sunshine, each hand grasping a berry basket. "Hmmm, smell the honeysuckle," said Irene. Bees buzzed by, already hard at their gathering task. Both girls closed their eyes, the better to feel the sun warm their faces. The sun bathed the farmhouse and barn and lit up the flowers planted around the house. Barefoot and barelegged, wearing flour sack dresses, the two sisters plunged into their morning's adventure. Irene, dark-haired and slender and one year younger than Bonnie, skipped along beside her fair-haired and slightly heavier sister. Both girls wore their hair neck-length, Irene's straight, Bonnie's tangled already.

"Let's go to the farthest place and watch for berries as we go, then turn around and gather them as we come back home," said Irene.

"What if bears get them first?" asked Bonnie.

"Silly, we don't have bears out here in Graham County."

"I know, just pretending. Maybe there will be Indians or escaped convicts, or animals escaped from a circus."

"The Jackrabbit Man would have to come a long way to get out here," said Irene.

"Yes, and Sheriff Hopkins said he would fill his britches with buckshot if he sees him again," said Bonnie.

"Well he escaped a week ago, but the paper says he probably headed for Canada or Mexico. How did he get to be called Jackrabbit?" asked Irene.

"Don't you know he bites the heads off jackrabbits and drinks their blood? Didn't you hear he swore to kill Sheriff Hopkins if he ever got out?"

"Sheriff Hopkins isn't afraid of anyone," said Irene.

"No, but we've got plenty of jackrabbits out here. Maybe that Mulloy wants to kill some jackrabbits and go after Sheriff Hopkins at the same time."

Irene shook her baskets at Bonnie. "Well, we better get going. Maybe Mr. Mulloy likes berries too."

The farm lay in the western part of Graham County, western Kansas, a few miles from Hill City, the county seat. They were too young to remember the tornado that destroyed Milbrook, the first Graham County seat. They had missed by several decades the last of the "Indian Troubles," when the Cheyenne dashed out of Oklahoma in a futile attempt to get into Canada, where they hoped to find a land of freedom and almost nabbed their Grandpa Fuller.

The girls vaguely remembered the prairie fire of 1913 that had all the Fuller and Morgan family fleeing for the Solomon River. Bonnie was a pill even then, at age four. As the family dashed for the river, Sheldon Bates (also known affectionately as Seldom Bates), a Negro boy from Nicodemus (founded in 1877 by newly-freed slaves) working for the family, asked where Bonnie was. Sheldon and Ray ran to the house and found Bonnie standing behind the front door. Sheldon and Ray each grabbed one of Bonnie's hands and rushed back towards the river.

"Now, why didn't you come out with the rest of us?" asked the father as they ran. "I wanted to watch the house burn down," she said. Ray shook his head in exasperation. "Umm, umm," said Sheldon, likewise shaking his head.

Grandpa Fuller, Louise's father, filled his children and grandchildren full of stories, some true, some doubtful, of his adventures as a cowboy for the Shiner Ranch in Texas and as a pioneer Kansas settler. Some of his children and grandchildren readily took up storytelling, sometimes for fun and sometimes to get out of trouble.

The South Fork of the Solomon River, fed by twenty or so small streams, crosses Graham County, making the area lush with flowers, berries and wildlife. The girls and their friends and siblings climbed and played under box elder and cottonwood trees that grew by the streams, and sometimes picked sunflowers, wild daisies, morning glories, and other small flowers. "But don't pick too many," advised their grandfather. "Especially don't pick any that grow close to the house."

The girls reached the end of the path to the dirt road that ran east and west, west to Penoke and east to Hill City. "Let's go around back of the house and head across the pasture into the woods," said Bonnie. "There are plenty of berry bushes around the edge of the woods."

"Not on your life," said Irene. Back of the house is the pig pen and you better not get caught anywhere near that pig pen."

"I already learned all the swear words I need," said Bonnie. "I don't need to turn loose the pigs again."

What the girls didn't know, what no one knew, except Ernest "Jackrabbit" Mulloy, was that Jackrabbit Mulloy had caught a Union Pacific boxcar bound for California. No one knew that Jackrabbit Mulloy planned to stop off near Hill City, slip into town and kill Sheriff Hopkins. He would then steal a car or hop a freight and head farther west. Mulloy figured that killing a sheriff would raise his prestige in the eyes of his criminal peers, who mainly regarded Mulloy with condescension and some embarrassment at being associated with the unlucky and at times hapless desperado.

Mulloy did not bite heads off jackrabbits to drink their blood. He got his nickname from an unlucky encounter with a bank customer who shot Mulloy in the leg during his attempt to rob the bank. The resulting injury caused Mulloy to incorporate a skip into his walk. Mulloy's associates in crime, seeing a chance for humor, and noting how well his limp went with his buck teeth, called him Jackrabbit. Mulloy himself had made up the story about biting heads off jackrabbits, hoping he would appear bloodthirsty and tough.

The Union Pacific crossed a trestle bridge less than five miles from the farm. The girls called the creek spanned by the bridge Solomon Creek. All the farm kids knew the risks involved in crossing railroad bridges. They knew at least two trains crossed the bridge during the day and two trains passed through during the night and early morning.

Each berry basket half-filled, hands and faces and dresses stained with red berry juice, for they could not resist tasting what they picked, Bonnie and Irene looked across the trestle. Blackberry and raspberry bushes grew in dappled sunlight around trees that grew by Solomon Creek. The girls didn't know that they were being watched, and cursed, by Jackrabbit Mulloy.

Mulloy had planned to cross the trestle in daylight and find a place to hole up until nightfall, when he would sneak into town and set fire to Sheriff Hopkins's home. With luck, Hopkins would be trapped inside. At the very least, Mulloy would strike some kind of blow against Hopkins. Truth was that Hopkins wasn't all that responsible for sending Mulloy to prison. He just happened to be Sheriff in Graham County when the posse captured Mulloy in his unsuccessful attempt to rob the Hill City Bank.

As the girls crossed the trestle, Mulloy slipped back farther into the woods. He found a depression surrounded by bushes and settled in. He noticed that some of the bushes sported blackberries or raspberries and gobbled down a handful. The prickly stems of the briars scratched his hands and face and Mulloy cursed silently to himself. Travel in the boxcar had covered Mulloy in dirt and even though Mulloy wasn't the cleanliest of men he was planning to immerse himself in the creek. Luckily for him the girls arrived when they did so he wasn't caught bathing in the creek.

Mulloy lay curled up in the depression; covered as best he could with brambles, dirty and tired and hungry and out of sorts because of scratches from the berry bushes. Gnats buzzed around the red juice from the berries that stained Mulloy's hands and face.

Bonnie and Irene hurried across the trestle bridge.

"We've got some time before the train comes through," said Irene. "Let's scout around for more berries."

Bonnie sat down at the end of the bridge. "Let's sit awhile. We're in no hurry. We'll be able to feel the vibrations in the rails so we'll know when the train is coming." Both girls sat down and soon, overcome by the warmth of the sun, stomachs filled with berries, they drifted off to sleep.

Jackrabbit Mulloy listened but didn't hear the girls talking. Mulloy was getting cramped in his hole and the stickers and gnats and other insects tormented him. "Maybe the little devils have left." Mulloy looked up and saw the sleeping girls. He cursed again but decided maybe he could sneak by them and cross the trestle. Anyway, if they saw him he could make up some story about being a hobo.

Mulloy crawled out of the hole with difficulty. His leg bothered him and he itched, wondering if there might have been some poison ivy in those bushes he hid in. The girls seemed to be fast asleep. Mulloy began to move towards the trestle and the sleeping girls.

Suddenly, Irene sat up. "What's that?"

Bonnie rubbed her eyes. "What?"

Irene pointed up the track. "The train's coming! I can feel the vibrations in the rails."

Bonnie grabbed her baskets and stood up. "We better skedaddle." Irene stood up too. At that moment, Mulloy tripped on a bramble and rose up from the brush, cursing and stained with berry juice.

"It's the Jackrabbit Man," screamed Bonnie.

"And he's killed a jackrabbit and drank its blood," said Irene. "Look at him."

The girls saw the red-stained face and hands of the escaped convict.

"That's right," yelled Jackrabbit Mulloy, "and you're next." He meant to scare the girls and that's what he did.

"Run!" And the girls ran away from Mulloy and onto the trestle bridge. "No! No!" Mulloy screamed. He didn't know what to do. He certainly wasn't going to kill any little girls, but he didn't want them to report him either. He didn't pursue them, however, because he saw the train coming.

"You girls get off that there trestle or you'll be ground up like sausage!"

The girls ran but they only made it to the middle of the bridge when Bonnie saw they would not be able to complete their crossing of the trestle before the train ran them down.

"Quick, Irene, under here." Bonnie pointed to an iron ladder that had been set there by trainmen for just such an occurrence in case they were caught on the bridge while doing repairs or inspecting track. Both girls scrambled down and clung tightly to the iron bars, baskets dangling from their arms, spilling precious berries. The roar of the train completely enveloped the girls. They clung there, alternately crying, screaming and even laughing once they realized they weren't going to die.

"Look, Bonnie." Irene pointed. "The Jackrabbit Man is running away." And that is what Mr. Jackrabbit Mulloy did. He forgot all about sneaking into Hill City and burning down the house of Sheriff Hopkins. Jackrabbit Mulloy figured that Graham County was just too unlucky for him.

Bonnie and Irene ran most of the way back home, pausing only to catch their breath. They ran into the house right up to their mother.

"The Jackrabbit Man, the Jackrabbit Man," both girls shouted. "He almost got us!"

Their mother looked down at both girls and shook her head. "Land sakes! You girls are getting to be as prone to tall tales as your Grandpa Fuller. And you've not got a full basket of berries between the two of you."

"No, no. He almost got us," said Irene. "He bit the head off a jackrabbit."

"And drank its blood," said Bonnie. "You could see it on his hands and face."

"Oh." Louise shook her head. "Looks like you bit the head off a jackrabbit your own selves. Pooh on the Jackrabbit Man. Go back out and get more berries."

As Bonnie and Irene left to complete gathering berries, Bonnie turned to her sister. "See, telling the truth doesn't do any good. It's best to make up a good story, like Grandpa."

Chapter 10

UNCLE AL IN EAST ARKANSAS

I was visiting my Uncle Al in Topeka so I could take him fishing at Shawnee County Lake. Uncle Al's time working as a carpenter had kept him fit over the years and even two hip replacements didn't slow him down very much. Being eighty-some years old with the two hip operations Uncle Al didn't drive anymore but he still had enough energy and strength to fish. He did wear a hat to protect his bald head from the sun and he did use a walker to make his way to where I had set up a lawn chair for him to fish from. Otherwise, Uncle Al was the same wiry, wispy-voiced, mischievous, bright-eyed idol of mine he had been since I was a lad. While my uncle checked through his tackle box and looked over his rods and reels I related my story about escaping a flash flood on the Gasconade River in Missouri. (River Memoir from River Memoir and other stories). When I asked Uncle Al if I could tape a story or two, he said "Sure, go ahead." He sipped from his coffee cup and began.

* * *

I never had any very stormy sessions fishing, but I used to go down into that swamp country in east Arkansas between the railroad and the highway, where they dug it out for the railroad. I hunted those big old swampers, swamp rabbits. They looked like our jack rabbits but down there they called them swamp rabbits. Damndest thing you ever seen. I'd shoot at them and they'd just jump in and swim across the swamp.

When I was a foreman at Fort Chafee before we got any prisoners, I was working six or seven Arkansawyers, two or three Oklahomans, and one guy from Kansas. I'd been working with them for awhile and one of the Arkansas boys, Henry, says, "Deer season's in, why don't you come down? When I asked where I would get a license the boy says, "Well, you just come down." So I said I would.

I drove down there one Friday night after work, planning to stay down there Friday and Saturday, then come back Sunday. I picked up a couple fifths of whiskey, good liquor, and planned to give it to them for their hospitality. I didn't know if they drank or not because there was never any drinking on the job and I always went right home after work.

The boys gave me directions, but I couldn't find their place. I'd stop and ask directions and no matter who I asked they all said, "Nope, never heard of him, must not live around here." So I kept going, thinking to myself, "Christ! Somebody must have heard of him."

I saw a little girl coming down the hill where I was stopped, trying to figure out where to go. I said, "Say, honey, can you tell me where Mr. Carr lives?" And she said, "Why yes, he lives on that first house right on top of the hill."

Dark was settling in when I drove up into the yard. One of the boys, Henry, came out and then another came out. It was a big house but all on one floor. I figured it must have six bedrooms in it, plus the kitchen and dining room and living room.

Henry says, "Mr. Fuller, I want you to meet my folks."
They was all there getting ready for suppertime and Henry
introduced me to about 21 of his family and in-laws. After
all the introductions were done I brought out the whiskey
I had got for them.

The old man says, "That's women's whiskey! Henry, get
the jug." So Henry brought out a jug and gave it to the old
man who uncorked it. The jug had never been opened.

The old man handed me the jug and I looped my index
finger through the neck ring and let the jug lie up against
my arm. Then I raised my elbow so I could tip the jug up
to my mouth and I took three big swallows and handed the
jug back to the old man. I couldn't talk, all I could do was
feel that moonshine burning down through my throat and
into my stomach.

"How do you like that?" asked the old man. "Brother," I
said, "That's a man's drink!"

Then they all took a sip, except for the women. I didn't
know it then, but they didn't allow their women to drink.
We sat around and talked a bit and then one of the women
said, "Supper's ready." We all sat around a big, long table
while some of the women waited on us.

I couldn't tell you how much stuff we had to eat. Why,
hell, the meat and potatoes and vegetables, and deer, and
any damn thing you could think of they had on that table.
And hot biscuits, the old lady had a clean apron on while
we were eating and she'd say, "Mr. Fuller, another biscuit?"
and I'd say, "I believe I will" and she'd reach into her apron
and give it to me. I had the best damn time down there I
ever seen. They just treated me swell.

The old man said, "I'll take you fishing, and I'll take you
hunting. We'll go deer hunting in the morning." So in the
morning we all piled into cars and trucks, the two brothers,

three brothers-in-law, the old man, me, and a couple other boys.

We'd come up to a place and the old man'd say to one of 'em, "Here's your spot." and further on to another, "All right, here's your spot," and so on. We finally came to a place where the old man says, "All right, Fuller, here's your spot. Have you ever gone deer hunting?" "No," I said. "Well," he said, "You get down into there, and don't you even smoke. You just sit there. When you hear those dogs hollering you'll know that the dogs have got a deer running."

I sat there for awhile and pretty soon I heard the dogs baying, first coming my way then veering off. A few minutes later I heard "Bang!" I sat there for another hour until they came by to pick me up. We went hunting again next morning, Sunday morning, and before we started off the old man says to me, "You know you aren't supposed to shoot nothing but a buck?" I said, "Sure." When they dropped me off this time the old man come up to me and says, "You just shoot the first deer you see." I said I probably would anyway because I couldn't tell them apart if they didn't have horns."

By god, one came my way and I shot and knocked it down. They all heard my gun go off so they came down there. "Where's your deer Fuller?" "He's down there," I said, pointing to where the deer was laying, about 30 yards off. "Why didn't you go down?" "I thought I might spook him if he was wounded and then I might lose him. I think it might have been a female." Well, they brought the deer up and it was a doe all right.

I said, "If I could have seen it was a doe I wouldn't have shot her. Don't we have to go down and report what we shoot?

"No, we have our own deer hunt here. They never come up to see what we shoot or nothing. They never bother us at all because they know we won't kill nothing but a buck and we won't take any more than we can eat."

When we went quail hunting the old man asked, "How many is in your family Mr. Fuller?" I said two and the old man said, "All right, get six quail and no more." He took me fishing and after I got me a nice mess of fish the old man said, "Ok, let's go home." The old man said, "Don't never shoot more meat than you can eat nor catch more fish than you can eat. Why waste it?"

I went about three times a year for four years before they took me to meet the moonshiner. I never asked to see the moonshiner. I figured there was nothing that would get me disinvited like asking anything about moonshiners.

One evening, after we had shot some quail Old man Carr threw half a dozen cleaned quail into a flour sack. He turns to me and he says, "How'd you like to meet our moonshiner?"

Well I was naturally curious to see his operation and to meet him too but I asked, "Are you sure that's all right?" Mr. Carr says, "If you're all right with me you're all right with anybody around these parts."

So we took off just as it was getting on toward dark. We went this way and that down some roads that would've been hard to find in daylight let alone dark, but Mr. Carr drove down them like they was his own driveway.

At last we come down some lane and the old man stopped the car. "You never want to just drive up to a house around here when you don't know the folks or they aren't expecting you." He looked hard at me. "Don't never come here on your own." Well I wasn't about to do anything that foolish, which is what I told Mr. Carr. "You know," Mr. Carr went on, "that's why no one would tell you where our place is. Ain't no one around here going to tell anyone not from around here anything. Sure, if you car breaks down they'll lend a hand but you probably won't never get their name."

Well I couldn't see nothing but the lane leading around some curve.

"Best to just wait here. They see our car lights. Another thing, you get lost going back to Fort Chaffee and need to stop for directions, don't never turn off your car lights and walk up to a house. If one of their dogs don't get you somebody might just shoot you. We just get out and stand so the lights show who we are."

Well we stood there, me smoking my Chesterfield and Mr. Carr smoking his Bull Durham hand rolled cigarette.

"Hey you old devil, who's that with you?" The voice came from behind and to the side. We turned to the voice and was blinded by the lights from our car. I guess that's what was intended.

"Why, Bill, this here's Mr. Fuller. The one that our boys work for at Fort Chaffee. We told you about him."

"Sure, come on ahead." We walked down the lane. I noticed that Bill kept behind us. A hundred yards or so we come to a pretty nicely built house, not as big as the Carrs but big enough so's a half dozen or so people could live there.

Mr. Carr said, "Fuller here thinks he can show you how to make better moonshine." Bill and Mr. Carr laughed at this and I did too even though that remark made me a bit nervous.

"Fuller brought some Jack Daniels down." Bill spat.

"Women's whiskey. Come on."

Well we walked a ways down the lane then Bill walked ahead a bit and cleared some brush that hid a path through the woods. We walked onto the path and Bill replaced the brush.

We walked on a bit more turning this way and that. I thought I spied a figure in the shadows sometimes but didn't say anything.

"Well here we are." Bill lit a lantern and sure enough sitting there was a beautiful piece of metal and pots and curved pipes. Even from up close the fire that boiled the makings didn't give off much smoke.

"Osage orange," explained Bill. "Burns long and hot. Good as coal."Well we stood around the still talking for awhile and then Bill said we better come up to the house and rest our feet. We sat there on the porch, me, Bill, Mr. Carr, and a couple of Bill's sons. Pretty soon, why, a woman come out with pie and coffee for each of us. We sat around talking about the war and eating our pie and sipping coffee.

Mr. Carr pointed a thumb at me. "Al here has a son in the Marines fighting Japs in the Pacific". Bill gestured towards his sons. "Can't let both of 'em go so they've got to draw straws to see which one joins up."

"Jubal here can fix anything that runs on gasoline but is only fair at hunting, which is what his brother Judah does best, but Judah is only fair at fixing motors and such."

Bill looked at me. "We're fixing to settle that question tonight. I'd like you to drive one of these boys to the signup place when you head back to Fort Chaffee."

We'd finished our pie and coffee and each of us had our coffee cup filled with Bill's white whiskey.

Bill lifted his cup. "We'll drink a toast to them that's fighting." We all tipped our cups and drank. "Now we'll drink a toast to him that's going." We all tipped our cups and drank again.

"All right Jubal, all right Judah take your pick." Bill held two straws in his closed fist. The brothers hesitated just a bit, then each drew a straw. Judah drew the short straw. He whooped.

"Hoo boy! Don't drink all the moonshine nor shoot all the deer while I'm gone."

"We'll save some for you," said Jubal. "Shoot us a Kraut or Jap where ever you get sent."

"Al, you'll take Judah to Fort Chafee so's he can sign up?"

So next morning I met Judah there at the trail leading to Bill's place and we drove back to Fort Chafee. This happened in the spring of '45. I heard later that with all the training there was Judah made it onto a troop ship but the war ended before he got anywhere.

Chapter 11

WORKING THE CHURCHES

by John Fuller, Edited by David Hann.
Recorded in June 1980

I was visiting my great uncle, John Fuller, in Topeka, where he and his wife, my Aunt Mamie, lived. I had recorded one of his stories and he asked me, "Would you like to hear one about the railroad?" Of course I said yes.

***

This was my first experience riding the rails. Your Uncle Earl and I was down in Kansas City and we shipped out on a railroad job that was in Caspar Wyoming by way of Billings, Montana. The next morning we went to the employment office and saw a job offered out at Senator Hogan's ranch. We went out there to see about it. Senator Hogan's bunkhouse was a log cabin, that was the bunkhouse. The spittoon was a hole about two feet wide in the floor. There were eight guys there besides us.

The next day, I and another guy, and Senator Hogan's wife, and his daughter went out to hoe beans. The ranch was right below the Rimrock in Montana. The Rimrock was a stop on the Great Northern Railroad then, and was named after sandstone cliffs that overlooked the valley. The

Senator ran cattle on the upper part and farmed on the lower part, see. We each took two rows up and two rows back and it was noon, two rows up and two back and it was supper time, night. That's how long they was, just two rows up and two back. You couldn't see the end of the row. Well, we done that for 4-5 days until harvest was ready.

The other kid quit and I was the only kid in a bunch of men. I was to shock the wheat. They made you wear leather boots up to your knee and leather gauntlets up to your elbows on account of rattlesnakes. This was August and the rattlesnakes were shedding and they were blind. They didn't rattle, they just struck. It was nothing to see some old boy, loading on the wagons, throw his pitchfork one way and he go the other way and there was a rattlesnake on the wagon with him. One time I climbed up on a wagon to help load and pulled myself up and there was a snake just two inches from my eyes and I looked right into the eyes of the snake. It was a bull snake, but that didn't help my pants any (laughs). I was the only kid there and worked there pert near two weeks. When I quit, the old boys that had killed a rattlesnake saved the rattles for me and gave me the rattles that they had cut from snakes they had killed. Everybody but me was above draft age in their forties or fifties, the only kid. The younger men had mostly gone off to World War I. When I quit I had a little better than a gallon bucket, half-full of rattlesnake rattles.

The boys would hook up a team of mules to a spring wagon whenever they was going into town. When I knew they was going into town I always let my whiskers grow for three days because there was a cop posted at every saloon to catch anyone who wasn't old enough. Hell, I'd go in with the rest of them and he never stopped me. At one saloon an old mountaineer, a trapper, had killed and skinned a rattler that was 18 inches across the middle and six feet long. The rattlers were round, about the size of a silver dollar.

After the wheat shocking was done at Senator Hogan's ranch Uncle Earl and I went to Great Falls, Montana to work at a smelter out there. I saw a small five ton weight fall on a guy and it him on the head. They found one foot and half of another one and what was left was just tissue paper. The dirt floor had been walked on so many years that it was hard as concrete. So I changed jobs and went to work at an arsenic plant. You worked five minutes at a time, wearing a hood with arm holes in it and a plexiglass visor. You didn't dare sweat, because then the arsenic would get into you and start eating on you and make sores. We had worked there two or three days. One Monday morning after I had worked two or three days, I went to work at one chamber. They had two big long screws, called augers, about 25 feet long and they had these canvas filters coming down above that shook the arsenic down into a railroad car called a gondola. They would load this gondola with the arsenic, see.

One of the screws broke so that left us with just one screw working. What we were doing, we had a little walkway there between the two screws. Our job was to shovel the arsenic into the screw that was operating and the arsenic would drop down into the gondola. A kid in his twenties, who had gotten married the day before, hadn't been out there an hour, and slipped into this auger and it ran up to his hip, before they got it stopped. Well, instead of getting the torch in there and cutting the auger they tried to knock the key out that held the auger in. That way they wouldn't need to shut down the arsenic line. The kid was white with arsenic, and sweating. The doctor was in there giving him one shot after another. Well, the key was rusted in and wouldn't budge. Every time they hit the pin, the kid hollered, and the doctor gave him a shot of morphine. They worked on him there for thirty-five minutes before they finally sent for the torch to cut him free. We never heard how the kid did and I had had all I wanted from that job so I quit.

After I quit the job at the arsenic plant, I went to work for the Great Northern there in Great Falls awhile. Then I went to Helena, Montana and worked for either the Northern Pacific or the Great Northern, one or the other. I worked there a couple of weeks. The room I rented had a tree with a limb that grew right close to my window. There was a popeyed magpie somebody had trained to talk. The magpie would come up there on that limb every day, just at daybreak and say, "Time to get up! Time to get up!" He wouldn't shut up until he saw me get up. I would have shot him if I had a gun.

I worked there for a couple of weeks and five other boys and I decided we'd go up and enlist. World War I was going on and we were ready for adventure. We goes up and I was the only one they took. There I was by myself.

After basic training I went to Fort Wright to be trained as a medic. Fort Wright was in Washington State just outside of Spokane. Some of us would go to field hospitals, some to secondary treatment centers and some would serve with the soldiers on the front lines. Because poison gas was being used we had gas mask tests all the time. Many a time I had a gas bomb go off near me during training and only had a few seconds to get my mask on. Going through that training saved my life several times later on because blood doesn't scare me.

We had to watch all operations. We got a guy name of Smith, who couldn't keep anything on his stomach. I and another medic in training took him into the operating room.

We held the glass and they give him this here white stuff they drink, you know? Of course, the doctor was standing there. We seen the drink move and pretty soon it stopped and the doctor said, "Well, that's where the knot is."

If that had happened today, they would have went in, taken a chunk out and sewed him up and he'd of been okay. All they could do at that time was take him back to the hospital and he died. So they had a post mortem.

There was thirty of us in there watching when they started. They made a cut around the head, so they could peel the scalp back from the skull. They cut the skull open with a saw and took the brain out. We lost four guys then. That left twenty-six of us. They cut the brain up and talked about it for awhile. They had a lady stenographer taking down everything the doctor said. Then they split across the top of chest, shoulder to shoulder and then cut right through the middle past his belly button. They peeled that back off his ribs. They cut the ribs and lifted them out and exposed all the insides.

The first thing they took out was his heart. When they got to that there was nineteen of us left. He whittled on the heart awhile, talking all the time and he got into the lungs and then there was fifteen of us left.

Then he comes down to the liver and we was having liver and onions that night for supper. The doctor is slicing on this liver, talking along, and he says, "Sergeant, go ask your cook if he's got enough liver for supper. There was three of us left then.

The doctor went ahead and finished his talking and the three of us edged around towards the door. The doctor said, "Now, sergeant, we're going to need two of these boys to sew him up." He lost the other three then. We took off. The sergeant went looking and found a kid named Pounds hiding under his cot. The sergeant found another kid, a very chunky kid named McDonald, who had tried to get out through a window. McDonald's belt buckle caught on a hinge on the window and he was just hanging there. Those two sewed him up.

Our trainers worked us hard so that we and any soldiers we took care of would have a better chance of surviving the war, which wasn't much of a chance if the newspapers could be believed. So with our hard training and the prospect of being in or near the trenches fairly soon my buddy Peters and I looked forward to our Friday evening liberty. We walked around downtown Spokane, passing by the bars and theatres and shops open late for us soldiers. We were standing on a street corner talking about what to do when two cute girls walked up to us.

"Hi boys, want to go to a party?"

First we just stared at them. Two cute girls being friendly to a couple of enlisted men? Peters responded immediately.

"Well that's very nice, thanks."

The girls explained that the party was being held in a tent just a few blocks away so we jumped at the chance. The girls led us into a big tent. We didn't hear any music or see anyone partying. We did see rows of chairs lined up before a podium.

"Just sit down here and we'll be right back." After Peters and I sat down the girls walked away. Several minutes passed and nothing was happening although we did see a few other girls escort young men, all servicemen, into the tent. Just as Peters and I were fixing to get up and go a man stepped up to the podium.

"God's blessing on everyone." A few people said "Amen" and then the preacher went to work. He condemned alcohol and dancing, and lewd behavior, the very things Peters and I were hoping to find at this so-called party. Then the preacher warmed to his work. He hammered away at sinners who were surely going to burn in Hell if they didn't forsake their evil ways and bad behavior. Several members of the crowd shouted "Amen" and "Praise God" and so forth.

Then came the big pitch. The preacher told everyone who was ready to be saved to raise their hands. Everyone in the crowd raised their hands except for Peters and me.

"I see some moral cowards in this blessed assembly, an assembly blessed by God the Almighty who is ready to take your poor sin-stained soul and make it shine like new."

A few heads turned our way because the preacher was looking right at us and pointing in our direction. Some nodded when the preacher repeated, "Moral cowards."

Peters and I showed the preacher what kind of cowards we were. We stood up and walked out of the tent with the preacher's promises of damnation and hellfire ringing in our ears. We passed by the two girls, now sitting at the back with their heads down, not looking at us. Peters stooped low to the nearest girl and said, "Lying is a sin, isn't it?" Her ears reddened but she kept her head down.

We were pretty steamed by being tricked and having our precious Friday evening liberty time shortened by those conniving girls.

We ambled down the sidewalk, ignoring the salesmen standing outside their shops trying to get us to "Buy that engagement ring for that girl back home." or "What you need is some good looking civilian clothes." whatever fool thing the fool salesmen thought they could push off on naive young servicemen.

"Two can play that game," said Peters. Then my buddy and I figured out a little racket we used to get home-cooked Sunday dinners. In those days there was no khakis. We wore our OD's, the enlisted man's dress uniform, every day. Sunday morning we'd put on our dress uniforms and take the early ferry across the bay to Spokane. We timed our arrival at churches right when they let out and we stood around the entrance as people filed out. Well, people naturally thought we'd been to their church service. Someone always asked us if we would like to come home with them to eat, and we naturally said we would be glad to go. That's what we were there for.

We worked all the churches in the south side of Spokane, not going to the same church twice for fear of being found out. This particular Sunday morning we decided to work the churches in north Spokane but we got to the church just a little late. We thought everyone had gone but, a man, his wife, and two daughters came out of the church just when we were fixing to leave. The man hollered at us and asked would we like to come home and eat dinner with them. That's what we were there for so we accepted.

Now one thing I didn't mention before was that we were short of everything at the base, including toilet paper. Well we always rolled up some whenever we visited our host's bathroom. We never took a whole roll, just wound several sheets around our fingers and stuck them into our belts in back.

Peters and I both had asked to use the bathroom, got our toilet paper wound up and stuffed behind our belts and sat around in our dress uniforms waiting for supper. The husband said, "Why don't you boys take off your jackets and get comfortable?" So we did. I turned around to hang my jacket on my chair and everyone burst out laughing. I couldn't think what it was they were laughing at. I reached around behind me and discovered three sheets of toilet paper hanging from my belt.

I had become so interested in talking to the girls that I forgot about the toilet paper. Peters began to put his jacket on but it was too late. More laughter and both my face and Peters was red as the cherry pie we had been eying. The family was nice about our little theft and insisted it was all right. We were so embarrassed that was the end of our church excursions. About a week later they shipped us to Camp Lewis, Washington. We got all our overseas shots and we were billed for Siberia. Another month and we would have been there, but the war ended.

Chapter 12

BARRY AND THE DEER

My friend, Barry Billings told me this story, saying "This could be the story of my life." I think he was talking about doing things without thinking them through.

My friend, Barry Billings told me this story, saying "This could be the story of my life." I think he was talking about doing things without thinking them through.

I had this idea that I was going to rope a deer, put it in a stall, feed it up on corn for a couple of weeks, then kill it and eat it. The first step in this adventure was getting a deer. I figured that, since they congregate at my cattle feeder and do not seem to have much fear of me when we are there (a bold one will sometimes come right up and sniff at the bags of feed while I am in the back of the truck not 4 feet away), it should not be difficult to rope one, get up to it and toss a bag over its head (to calm it down) then hog tie it and transport it home.

I filled the cattle feeder then hid down at the end with my rope. The cattle, having seen the roping thing before, stayed well back. They were not having any of it. After about 20 minutes, three deer showed up. I picked out a likely looking one, stepped out from the end of the feeder, and threw my rope. The deer just stood there and stared at me. I wrapped the rope around my waist and twisted the end so I would have a good hold. The deer still just stood and stared at me, but you could tell it was mildly concerned about the whole rope situation. I took a step towards it...it took a step away. I put a little tension on the rope and then received an education.

The first thing that I learned is that, while a deer may just stand there looking at you funny while you rope it, they are spurred to action when you start pulling on that rope. That deer EXPLODED.

The second thing I learned is that pound for pound, a deer is a LOT stronger than a cow or a colt. A cow or a colt in that weight range I could fight down with a rope and with some dignity. A deer? no chance. That thing ran and bucked and twisted and pulled. There was no controlling it and certainly no getting close to it. As it jerked me off my feet and started dragging me across the ground, it occurred to me that having a deer on a rope was not nearly as good an idea as I had originally imagined. The only upside is that they do not have as much stamina as many other animals. A brief 10 minutes later, it was tired and not nearly as quick to jerk me off my feet and drag me when I managed to get up. It took me a few minutes to realize this, since I was mostly blinded by the blood flowing out of the big gash in my head.

At that point, I had lost my taste for corn-fed venison. I just wanted to get that devil creature off the end of that rope. I figured if I just let it go with the rope hanging around its neck, it would likely die slowly and painfully somewhere. At the time, there was no love at all between me and that deer. At that moment, I hated the thing, and I would venture a guess that the feeling was mutual. Despite the gash in my head and the several large knots where I had cleverly arrested the deer's momentum by bracing my head against various large rocks as it dragged me across the ground, I could still think clearly enough to recognize that there was a small chance that I shared some tiny amount of responsibility for the situation we were in. I didn't want the deer to have it suffer a slow death, so I managed to get it lined back up in between my truck and the feeder—a little trap I had set beforehand ... kind of like a squeeze chute. I got it to back in there and I started moving up so I could get my rope back.

Did you know that deer bite? They do! I never in a million years would have thought that a deer would bite somebody, so I was very surprised when I reached up there to grab that rope and the deer grabbed hold of my wrist. Now, when a deer bites you, it is not like being bit by a horse where they just bite you and then let go. A deer bites you and shakes its head almost like a pit bull. They bite HARD and it hurts.

The proper thing to do when a deer bites you is probably to freeze and draw back slowly. I tried screaming and shaking instead. My method was ineffective. It seems like the deer was biting and shaking for several minutes, but it was likely only several seconds. I, being smarter than a deer (though you may be questioning that claim by now) tricked it. While I kept it busy tearing the bejesus out of my right arm, I reached up with my left hand and pulled that rope loose.

That was when I got my final lesson in deer behavior for the day. Deer will strike at you with their front feet. They rear right up on their back feet and strike right about head and shoulder level, and their hooves are surprisingly sharp. I learned a long time ago that, when an animal like a horse strikes at you with their hooves and you can't get away easily, the best thing to do is try to make a loud noise and make an aggressive move towards the animal. This will usually cause them to back down a bit so you can escape. This was not a horse. This was a deer, so obviously, such trickery would not work. In the course of a millisecond, I devised a different strategy. I screamed like a woman and tried to turn and run.

The reason I had always been told NOT to try to turn and run from a horse that paws at you is that there is a good chance that it will hit you in the back of the head. Deer may not be so different from horses after all, besides being twice as strong and three times as evil, because the second I turned to run, it hit me right in the back of the head and knocked me down.

Now, when a deer paws at you and knocks you down, it does not immediately leave. I suspect it does not recognize that the danger has passed. What they do instead is paw your back and jump up and down on you while you are lying there crying like a little girl and covering your head. I finally managed to crawl under the truck and the deer went away.

So now I know why when people go deer hunting, they bring a rifle with a scope so that they can be somewhat equal to the Prey.

Chapter 13

ED ROSETTA

One snowy Sunday winter afternoon I talked friend Terri Tork into joining me in a sixty-some mile drive to Osage City, Kansas, where I hoped to meet with a former coal miner who had worked mines in Osage County.

The snow that had been falling all day turned to sleet as we arrived at the small eastern Kansas town. Although the four hundred or so homes and 1,000 or so inhabitants of Osage City would be regarded as average for Kansas, Osage City and surrounding towns had a history that belied the image of Kansas cow towns. Mining had been an important part of Osage County's income for almost one hundred years at the time of my journey to Osage City. Between 1885 and 1934 at least 144 mining deaths occurred in the course of Osage operations.

A friend in Lawrence suggested I contact Mr. Ed Rosetta, who ran an antique shop in Osage City. When we arrived at the address given for the antique shop we found it had been turned into a western wear store. Women there informed us that the antique store had been closed for two or three years, but one of the women was Mr. Rosetta's grand-daughter-in-law. The other woman was his great-granddaughter-in-law. They called Mr. Rosetta and told him we were interested in talking to him about the mines. Mr. Rosetta said to come on over. He would be willing to talk with us.

The sleet hissed through the tree limbs in front of Mr. Rosetta's home. We could see it reflected in his porch light. Mr. Rosetta greeted us at the door and said to hang our coats over chair backs in the kitchen. We brushed the sleet from our coats and boots and went in. Mr. Rosetta had a pot of coffee going and he sat steaming cups down in front of us. His wife stayed in the living room seated on the sofa. Mrs. Rosetta had been ill recently and spent a lot of time resting on the sofa.

Mr. Rosetta wore overalls over a flannel shirt. His grey hair was thick and curly, his hands big with thick, strong-looking fingers. You could tell this man had led a laborer's life.

I told Mr. Rosetta that my interest in coal mining came from reading about a mine rescue that took place in 1874 and that I had decided to learn more about mining in Kansas. Mr. Rosetta had not heard of the incident I spoke of, but my interest prompted him to relate some of his experiences in the mines around Osage City. Those accounts turned into Mr. Rosetta giving us his life story, related below as he told it.

✳✳✳

It was about this time of year, if I'm not mistaken, around November, maybe December. It was getting pretty close to Christmas, 1916. I had an experience of taking a couple of fellows out of a mine burning, right down here, just about three blocks right straight north. That was mine number 7, run by Sam Carlin.

I came to work one morning. I was about 17, 18 years old. It was dark. You know how it is in the wintertime. We go to work at 7:30 in the coal mines, and I always liked to be up there around 7:00. As I approached the mine I could see a light. It would flicker and then go out. Then it would come on again, then flicker and go out. When I got up real close I could see that the tipple had burned down clear to the ground. At mine number 7 the tipple was just a small shack where the coal was heisted up to be sorted and load-ed onto a truck.

I knew two men were working down there. I went across, about a block and one-half, to a neighbor who lived close to the mine. I woke him up and told him to put in an alarm. So, I went running back to the mine. There were a lot of people gathered down there. The only way we could go down there was the escape hole. You see, they've got a main hole, for heisting the coal with the tipple. Then they have an air hole you can come up to escape, quite a ways off from the main hole. That's the way we went down, using the steep, wooden stairway.

Three of us went down. The smoke was so bad that we couldn't approach. We had to retreat back some ways. I said, "I know those boys are in here. There's only one thing to do." I ripped my shirt off. I always wore a cotton shirt to work in. I tore strips from my shirt and soaked them in a bucket of water. You always carry water to the mine. Then we tied the rags around our faces. Our eyes would smart, but we got 'em. We brought them up to the escape hole and had a rope to heist them up from there. We got them on top, but they were gone.

If they'd had more experience in coal mines, they might have made it. If those boys would have known, because if you don't panic and use your head, why, they could have laid flat on the ground of the entry. You know what an entry is? That's the road that you go into the coal fields and back out to the bottom and all, and then there's a cut, road heads where you could dig out the coal.

But they panicked and they was trying to go around the mine to get on the other side of it and they knowed, if they could make it to that air cave they'd have been safe, you see, cause the air was coming down there and throwing air around the mine. But they didn't do it. We found them in the place where I worked. One of 'em, they were half-brothers, one of 'em was up about fifty feet ahead of the other. You could see one fellow probably would have made it if he hadn't stayed back and tried to help his brother.

When he went out he crawled fifty feet more and he was gone, exhausted. Smoke got 'em, killed them both.

My brother had just come out of the mine. The ten o'clock shift. They were working three shifts around the clock in the coal mines. They had two persons to the shift. They were driving what they call a tight entry. You don't know what a tight entry is, but it's a driver that goes ahead and makes rooms to make more places to dig out the coal. They were driving that in. They only had about the width of this room. They would turn rooms off the wall. And that's what happened.

They were working three shifts around the clock. But, they should've had a night watchman. Now there's a law to have a night watchman on top. That was ridiculous. To send two men down there and leave them there without anybody on top. And you couldn't sue the man, the owner. He didn't have anything other than a little old tipple coal mine. Now, you see, they have a night watchman on top. They have to. That's the law.

No one knows why the tipple caught on fire. It could have been a bad wire, maybe something rubbing inside. They always leave a fire going in the stove on top, too, banked so there would be something going the next morning. It caught someways, a spark or something. Unlucky for the two boys.

I had a lot of experiences in the coal mines. I was in them coal mines forty years, more or less. I think I was about thirteen, maybe fourteen years old when I went down. I didn't want to go to school anymore. My dad, he wanted me to go to college. I wouldn't listen. I wanted to go to work and make a lot of money. You didn't make very much money in those days, a couple of dollars a day, dollar and a half. You had to be a pretty good man to make that kind of money in those days. We worked eight hours a day.

Years before that, my dad worked in coal mines though I didn't know it. I was just a boy then, just a boy. We lived on a farm and he was here in town. We never did see him. I remember that he came home one time and I asked my mother who that fellow was. She said, "Why that's your father, boy. What are you talking about?" I said, "I don't know. I never did see him."

They worked at night. In the daytime they had to load the coal in buckets at the bottom, you see. They had to wait on the turn. They didn't have a crew to mine the placer. Then at four o'clock they closed down and went to mine the placer. They worked day and night to make a living. They were putting in sixteen hours a day. There wasn't a union in those days. It was grab as grab can, you see.

I never went through those circumstances, but my dad did. He had his back broken in a coal mine and that's what killed him. He died a pretty young man, sixty-six years old. They didn't know anything about it in those days you know. His circulation never returned. His blood turned to water and he died anemic.

I've helped take a lot of them out of there, smashed up, dead, alive, this and that. I got caught one time in a cave in. I was lucky. I barely got my head out of the way. The falling rock tore all the ligaments loose in my legs. I still have a knot on my leg from that cave in. I never got a dime for my injury. I was off work quite awhile and they never gave me a nickel.

That's the way it is. That's poor man's luck. I was living in Burlingame. That would make it 1921 or 1922. I was married in November and had a girl baby when that happened. You know, me and that woman in there, on the 8th day of November, we had been married 59 years. I lived in Burlingame a couple of years. I was in the Army 880 days. Outside of that I've been here. Oh, I went to Lexington, Missouri, to work in that coal mine. I went to Iowa and worked in those coal mines. All rat holes, ha, ha, ha. Possums wouldn't live down in the mines.

The last coal mine closed around here twenty-five years ago, more or less. There's a few strippers around here. You know, that's on top. They strip the coal from the top. Well, nobody burns coal anymore. Now they're going back to burning wood. They may have to go back to burning coal the way this gas shortage is going.

It's been nip and tuck, my life. I finally got lucky. You know there's a black lung pension that was going around a few years ago. I didn't want to apply for it and that woman there said, "You're foolish if you don't. You'd be surprised what you can get out of it." So I signed up and after I went out there, they turned me down. I just made up my mind then that we were going to fight. They said they didn't have enough evidence, you see. They had to take X-rays of your lungs.

Your lungs clear up after being out of the mine for awhile. Of course I had seen my lungs, what they looked like. I quit the coal mines in 1950. In the spring I came out. We don't work in the mines in the summertime around here, only in the wintertime when it's cold. We were off about four or five months in the summertime.

And, I went up and got a job in 1950 at the supply depot in Topeka. You know, there's a supply depot that was on the west side of the road. On the east side of the road was the army base. I went up there and started working up there in 1950. In the year 1951, they would come down there with a machine that takes X-rays of your lungs. They took the X-rays to check for tuberculosis. Not only for coal miners, but everybody. You had to take the tests and they didn't cost anything. The government pays for that. So, I went and had my chest examined and I went home.

I came home from my job in Topeka one night in 1951. We were living in this house. I came into the house and she was in there crying. I asked, "What's the matter with you? What happened?" She had a letter in her hand and she held it out to me. "Read this letter," she said. "You'll find out what happened." I read the letter. It was from some doctor in Topeka, about the X-rays I had taken. The doctor said in the letter, "Mr. Rosetta, we want you to come to Topeka immediately. We don't know how you live with lungs like you have."

I knew exactly what the trouble was. I had been in the mines for forty years, more or less. In the coal mine you not only inhale the dust of the coal mine, but dynamite fumes, carbide lamp fumes, everything. Sometimes, black damp forms where the air can get in. That's deadly poison. And you have to compete with all of them.

So, there was nothing to do but go up and see the doctor. His office was south of the dome, at the capitol in Topeka. My sister-in-law took me up. She couldn't find any parking place around so she said, "I'll let you off here, on the north side. Take your time. I've got to go downtown and do a little shopping. Then I'll come back and pick you up." I said, "When I get done I'll come by here and sit down where you let me off." She said, "Okay."

I had to go through the dome. I went through the capitol and went in to the place there and I had to go clear
down to the south side of the dome. That's where the doctor was. And, ahh, there, as I was approaching the dome, I
never did see such a commotion in all my life. Somebody
was working up there with scaffolding, iron scaffolding and
planks, that kind of thing. A piece of scaffolding fell and I
jumped out just in time. I came pretty near getting killed
right there. So I kind of got shocked. I froze.

People came out there wanting to know what happened.
I said, "Well I don't know. I would say that God loves the
Italians. I came pretty near to getting killed here. It's about
as close as I want to see it."

Well, anyhow, I went around the dome and I went in
and I found the doctor's office, where I had to go. I went
in and he says, "What can I do for you mister?" I said, "It's
not what you can do for me, it's what I can do for you." I
throwed him that letter, down there. And he picked it up
and said, "Oh my god, yes!" Then he got that X-ray and
throwed it down. Every bit of my lungs was black. There
wasn't a white spot on them.

I looked at it for awhile and kind of laughed. I said,
"That's awful ain't it? Isn't that the most awful looking thing?
It's a hell of a world for a person to get in that shape." The
doctor sat there and got kind of mad. He said, "What the
hell kind of man are you, laughing at something like that?
I've never seen a man with lungs like that. Why, if I had
lungs like that, I'd get something done."

I just kept joking with him and the more I joked with
him the madder he got. Finally I told him. I says, "Doc,
did you ever doctor a coal miner in your life?" And he
says, "No, I never did." And I said "That's just what that is.
I'm fresh out of the mines. I just came out of there in the
spring. That's the reason it's still there. It'll clear up in time.

I coughed and spit up a chunk big as my thumb. "Is that the case of it?" the doctor said. "Well, how can you live?" I said, "I've lived forty years with it. It clears up in time." He said, "Your lungs will be severely damaged." I said, "I know a lot of them at home that can't breathe. They get pretty old and they call it the miners' asthma."

But here now they have a different name for it. They call it the black lung. They put a big name to it. It's about that long. (Mr. Rosetta spread his arms out to either side.) You'd have to chop it up into a hundred pieces in order to swallow it."

The doctor says, "Well I don't see how you can live."

I said, "Well, doc, people live to be some ninety years old, working in the mines. I know several down there. I don't worry about that. It's damaged my lungs, no question about it, but as you go along, why, that will clear up."

I was up there ten years getting treated for black lung before the program closed down and I got my pension out of it. I had ten of those X-rays taken. I wish I had known then that we was going to go up for this black lung thing coming in, you know.

If I would have got those X-rays earlier I wouldn't have had any trouble getting my pension anyhow. They kept refusing and I kept asking. I fought back. They turned me down and I'd renew it. I wouldn't wait until tomorrow. I'd go up there and keep fighting them. They had me go everywhere. It never cost me anything to go up and get the X-rays. The government paid for it.

Then finally one day they sent me a letter. It said, "Mr. Rosetta, we don't have quite enough evidence to give you this black lung pension, but we suggest you go to a doctor of your choosing. And we advise you to go to your family physician. If he's been doctoring men with black lung he knows."

And I went down to Dr. Williams, here in Osage City, and told him I got to have an examination and he said, "Come on down here and I'll give it to you." He got quite a bit of money for doing that. So he says, "I can't give it to you in the daytime, because I'm awfully busy. You come down about 7 o'clock at night. We'll do the job."

So I went down there one night at 7 o'clock. And I stayed there outside of his office for about an hour and a half, cold, snow was on the ground. I turned the car on to get a little heat, then turn it off for awhile. Finally, he came out waved me to come in and he gave me an examination. It was about an hour and a half. He asked me a lot of questions. Wrote down everything on a piece of paper. But he kept going back to one of these lungs over here. He'd go back and then he'd shake his head. Then he'd go over there and then he'd come back over here again. He kept doing that, and he'd write all that down.

He got my pension for me. He evidently found something wrong. And I noticed there was something wrong. I don't have any wind. I used to like to go hunting and fishing but I had to cut it all out. I'm eighty-two years old, you know, eighty-two years old and I'll be eighty-three the second day of February. I'm a groundhog.

That's the way it is in life. I worked in many of those holes. I even went down to Pleasanton, Kansas one time, and worked down there awhile, and Lexington, Missouri. There was coal there and the coal was thicker but there was more dirt on top of the coal. We had to have a face tract. You'd run the coal right along the track. You'd load the coal. You didn't have to kick it out to the road heads. Kicking it out means you work lying down in a space twenty inches wide. You dig out the coal and kick it out. Here, you have to kick it out to the road head. And they'd load it from the road head. We got rails. They went into your place. We called them rooms. This was small coal, average about fifteen inches. Now in Burlingame, we'd have a little bigger coal. They had around sometimes twenty inches, sometimes twenty-two inches of coal.

But the biggest coal I ever worked into, we went to Cartersville, Iowa. And when I went in there to look at that mine, you know, when you're used to working in coal fifteen inches and this was four-foot veins. That's an awful lot of coal there, you know. Yeah, I didn't care too much for it. I can make more money down here. I'm used to working in these little pencil markings. But they all have difficulty. They all have that background.

There aren't any old mines around here. The dumps are still here. I could show you the dumps. I could show you dumps after dumps. That's where they put all the dirt. And there's a dump out here where I told you. And I hauled out a lot of that dirt there. The last coal mine I worked in here, I worked on a mine by the highway, on the way to Admire. There's a coal mine there on the left hand side of the road. I put a lot of dirt over there, too. They look like mountains. That's what they look like, big piles of dirt. You can tell by the color of it too. Did you ever see a coal dump? We've got a lot of them around here.

The black lung pension originated from where all those men got killed in that mine up there in Pennsylvania. Close to 100 people got trapped and killed. You probably read about it. Some of the boys here who have been trying to get on haven't got it yet. They get letters saying their request is out of order. Then they send them letters to renew their requests.

I got back pay for two years. One day after I went to that doctor who got my black lung pension for me, I was on retirement then. That was, let's see, seven or eight years ago. Now, see, when I was a little boy I took home my earnings in an envelope. A letter came in the fifth day of February. And my wife knew that the pension came in on the third. And she says "I think you've got your black lung pension." She handed me the envelope and I was just shocked. I just stood there a little, shocked. My wife says, "Aren't you going to open it?" I said, "I guess I will," and took out my pocketknife and opened it. Sure enough, there was a check in there. It just lacked eighty-some dollars of being $6,000 of back pay. Then after that I started getting a pension every month, $249. Now it's $300 and some due to cost of living.

We've been one of the luckiest...We went through hell a lot of our days until the Second World War. I worked up at the supply depot long enough to get a pension out of there. It was awfully small to begin with, $57, but now it's up to $175. With the pension and the social security we're doing all right. Of course on the other hand, time is running out because I'm 82 years old. Still, I'm getting something from all that dirty coal mining yet, pretty lucky.

We've been through a lot of hell, pardon me, but the Bible uses it. We've been through a lot of rough times, I can tell you that. We raised a girl up there. She finally got married. We didn't buy her any clothes. We never did have the money. She always wore hand-me-downs, and she never complained. She gives away clothes now, beautiful clothes. I asked her, "Why don't you do what those others do? Have a garage sale." She said, "Daddy, remember when people used to give them to me? I haven't forgotten that." We've only got the one girl and she's worth a million, a wonderful girl. We wouldn't know what we'd do if we didn't have her.

Well, I wish you would have been here some time when we was digging and seen me come home when I was covered with coal dust and ragged as a beggar. There's just a few of us now. You could count us on fingers of one hand.

***

I raised my cup and thanked Mr. Rosetta. He had been talking for about two hours. I thought he might be short of breath and didn't want to wear him out by staying longer. Terri thanked him and turned to Mrs. Rosetta and thanked her too. "Thanks for coming all this way," she said. Mr. Rosetta said, "You young folks be careful on the road." Sleet rattled against the windows. We slipped on our coats, scraped off the windshield and drove back to Lawrence in the icy night, talking about our good fortune in meeting Mr. Ed Rosetta.

PART III - THE MARINE CORPS

I enlisted in the Marines in September, 1963, at age nineteen and served three years in what a Marine commandant described at "the most agile of our fighting forces." After basic training in boot camp at MCRD San Diego and four weeks of ITR (Infantry Training Regiment) at Camp Pendleton, and several months electronics training at San Diego I began my real service at Camp Pendleton, Electronics Maintenance Company, 1st Force Service Regiment. In August, 1965 I joined the rest of our company in a voyage to Okinawa. After several months trying I finally got my orders to go to Vietnam, with only seven months left in my enlistment. I returned to the U.S. in September, 1966, and was discharged a few days after returning to The World, as we called the U.S. 66

Chapter 14

YELLOW FOOTPRINTS

Marines know what it means to stand on those yellow footprints. I came close to never knowing. Bishop Miege High School friend Richard Glenner came by to visit fresh from Marine Corps boot camp. Rich enlisted in the Marine Corps after trying one semester of college. He was tanned and fit and full of stories about the rigors of boot camp and infantry training.

High school friends Steve Kidwell and Mike Thoennes (pronounced tennis) and I listened with interest. The three of us had completed our freshman year at college but realized we weren't ready. What to do?

I worked at SEQUAL, a sheet metal fabrication shop in Kansas City. Kidwell worked at his father's service station. Thoennes was looking. None of us saw a future in our current situation.

Here was Rich Glenner, who had taken the big step. We were in pretty good condition from playing sandlot baseball, basketball, football, or maul the man with the ball when we didn't have enough kids for a game. We also lifted weights. I only weighed 105 pounds but I could lift that weight over my head. We talked it over amongst ourselves, enlisted, then told our families.

When I announced my decision at dinner, my sister

Sharon visiting from Minnesota said, "I think you've made a big mistake. You should stay in school."

"I'm not doing very well in school. I'm just wasting my time."

My younger brother Doug shook my hand. My mother asked if I was sure and my father said I was getting into the roughest, toughest, meanest outfit there was. He might have been thinking about Cousin Lauren, who was a Marine veteran of World War II and Korea. Lauren had been infamous for brawling with sailors before he settled down. Another cousin, "Rip" Althoff, had married into our family and was at that time a Marine sergeant.

He advised, "Keep your sense of humor and give your soul to God because the Marine Corps' got your ass."

Uncle John, who had been a medic during World War I recommended, "Pay attention. Listen hard to your trainers."

I remembered and usually followed all this advice once I finally became a recruit, but there was an unseen obstacle to me getting in.

Departure day came. Steve's brother Don drove us to the recruiting office in downtown Kansas City, grinning as he departed, "When you come back I'll call you men."

We lined up to take the oath. Before we began, a sergeant walked up and said, "David Hann?" I raised my hand.

"I'm sorry, David, the Marine Corps can't take you. Your vision doesn't meet the minimum requirements for enlistment."

I heard another sergeant say, "He sees fine up close but at 400 yards he's almost blind without his glasses."

That was true sure enough. I inwardly cursed my weak eyes. The sergeant led me to an office. I could only stand there speechless, deflated. I heard the oath of enlistment being given and repeated by Kidwell and Thoennes and other recruits in the next room.

Sergeant White, looked at me.

"There is a chance. You could apply for a waiver to be admitted even though you don't pass the vision requirement."

"I'd like to apply for the waiver."

Sergeant White pulled out a form, made a few notations and slid it to me. I signed.

"While you're waiting to hear back, try going without your glasses as much as possible."

I returned home shaken and disappointed. My family may have been relieved but I, the 4F, was miserable. I returned to my job at SEQUAL and I continued to exercise, including weight lifting.

One day I began practicing dead lifts but I didn't warm up first. A dead lift involves standing and touching your toes except you hold a weight, in my case a 60 lb. barbell, then you bend down and touch the floor with the weight. I felt muscles in my lower back stretch like taffy being pulled. I did a few more dead lifts thinking it best to keep working out. Next day my back was very sore. From then on standing or walking on a level hard surface made my back feel like the spine was grasped by vice grips.

I kept pumping aspirin and that helped, that and the fact I was young. A few weeks later, while working at SEQUAL I got a phone call from the recruiting office.

"Phone call for Lieutenant Commander Hann," yelled one of my co-workers. It was Sgt. White.

"Your request was approved. Be down here Monday morning."

Again I said goodbye to my family, shaking my father's hand again and him wishing me luck. I don't remember who drove me to the recruiting office but once there I met a handful of other recruits and we took the oath. Sgt. White drove us to the airport and we boarded the plane. Before we left him Sgt. White advised, "Whatever that sergeant orders you to do, do it as quickly as you can."

We recruits talked a little about where we expected to be assigned after boot camp and infantry training, what boot camp might be like, how much fun we would have learning to fire all kinds of weapons. Even though we were eager, all of us were a bit subdued. We knew we were in for tough training.

I guess there were about twenty of us at the airport, coming from states west of the Mississippi. Recruits east of the Mississippi went to Paris Island. We were called Hollywood Marines because our boot camp was at Marine Corps Recruit Depot (MCRD) San Diego.

Many of my soon-to-be platoon mates wore their hair long. One recruit, a Cajun from Louisiana, in particular stood out to me because of his thick, bushy hair. Some recruits wore duck tails, a popular hair style in the early sixties.

A truck, which we would later know as a 6X6, or 6 By, pulled up. A Marine sergeant got out, holding a clip board.

"When I read your name get on the truck. No loud talking."

In a few minutes we were on the truck and heading for MCRD, which would be our home for the next 13 weeks. I don't recall that anyone spoke. We pulled up to Receiving Barracks. The sergeant got out and stood by the truck.

"Get out and stand at attention on the yellow footprints. No talking without permission."

We tumbled out of the truck and stood at attention on the yellow footprints. Were we tense? You bet.

Three Marines stood before us now, a sergeant, and two corporals.

"The first word out of your skuzzy mouths will be 'Sir.' You will say 'Yes Sir' to any order and then do it immediately."

"Do you understand?" This was addressed to me and I said, "Sir, yes."

"Sir, yes," repeated the corporal scornfully. He took a drag on his cigarette and blew smoke into my face.

One by one we were directed to run into the building and sit in the barber's chair. The barber shaved us down to the scalp with a few swipes of his clippers.

We ran about in fear and confusion, getting rid of clothes, showering, donning what would be our uniform for the next thirteen weeks, sateen green utilities, called fatigues or dungarees in the Army but in the Marine Corps they were called utilities. Green shirt, green pants, green hat, called a cover in the Marine Corps, black boots, black socks, beige web belt, shirt buttoned to the neck, pants let down to ankle level, covers crammed onto heads, we only waited moments for the next order.

Assembled once again, shorn and suited in green we stood at attention. A sergeant we would know as Drill Instructor (DI) Sgt. Camp instructed us how to march and gave us the order to march.

"Owl aye owl!"

What was that? It was Sgt. Camp, calling out cadence, meaning "Left right left" that from Sgt. Camp came out like "Owl aye owl!" Each DI had his own distinct way of counting cadence. The cadence comes from personal preference on the part of the DI and also from practical necessity so that a platoon could identify their DI's cadence from another's. Our Platoon Gunnery Sergeant, Gunnery Sergeant Berger, simply called out "Left right left." Sgt. Rhine's cadence went "Aye aye aye."

We marched to our Quonset huts, structures that looked like giant aluminum barrels lying on their sides. I lay at rigid attention on my bunk bed, which forever after would be known as a rack, and somehow slept.

I endured my first morning in boot camp in a trance. I think most of us were numbed by shock. Sgt. Camp marched us to the mess hall and told us, "No talking. You've got ten minutes to eat and be standing at attention outside."

Later on we got a few more minutes to eat but this first shortened time limit impressed upon us the importance of eating and getting out.

We gulped down our breakfast and dashed outside with our metal trays and flatware, scraped off leftovers, dumped the trays into boiling soapy water, then boiling clean water to rinse, then added the trays to a stack. In the future we were so hungry that leftovers were seldom seen. The trays and flatware would be washed again but we had to go through the exercise. We didn't know it but we were learning to be responsible for everything we touched.

Much to our surprise the first thing Sgt. Camp taught us was how to make our beds, or racks, to the satisfaction of our DIs.

Sgt. Camp selected four of the taller recruits to hold up the metal bed frame with its bare mattress. He then went through the process of making up the rack. Tight sheets, tight blanket, done just so. The morning grew warmer and I felt sweat run down the middle of my back.

Lesson over, Sgt. Camp marched us to what would be our home for five weeks, after which we would go to the rifle range for four weeks, then back to the Quonset huts for the last four weeks, those of us who survived that long.

Bunks made, Sgt. Camp assembled us outside our three Quonset huts, each of which held 25 or so of the 75 recruits that comprised Platoon 174, 1st Battalion, Marine Corps Recruit Depot San Diego (MCRD).

Sgt. Camp quickly arranged us into four rows, tallest at the head of each row, thereafter referred to as 1st squad, 2nd squad, 3rd squad, and 4th squad. Sgt. Camp appointed

the first man in each squad as the Squad Leader. Being 5'5"
I was towards the end of the 1st squad. I was surprised to
find there were two or three recruits just a bit shorter than
me. Because of the alignment according to height, DIs referred to the rear of the squad as the little end.

"This is your position in the platoon. You will not change
your place in the squad or place in the platoon unless ordered to do so by a DI. Is that clear?"

A low "Yes Sir." came in response.

"I CAN'T HEAR YOU, GIRLS!"

We responded much louder, "YES SIR."

Sgt. Camp read our names and we yelled in reply, "Sir,
Pvt. _____ here, sir."

Roll call over, Sgt. Camp ordered us back into our
Quonset huts to stand at attention in front of our racks. He
said that whenever a Drill Instructor entered the Quonset
hut someone better sound out, "Attention!" Sgt. Camp then
growled, "At ease. That means you remain standing, however. I better not catch anyone sitting down."

Sgt. Camp left and we stood around our racks, thirsty
but with no water in sight. We whispered to one another,
not knowing what might come next.

"What do you think we'll do next?"

"When will they issue us guns?" We quickly learned to
never refer to our rifles as guns.

"I wonder if we can go to the bathroom." We learned to
call the bathroom or toilet "the head."

I discovered that I was not issued a shelf that fit onto
ledges built into the foot locker. Sgt. Camp had told us to
contact him if there were problems with our issue. I did not
want to attract any attention but I had to tell Sgt. Camp I
needed the shelf. I ran to the Duty Hut, the DIs office. I
felt like I was entering the gates of Hell.

"BAM! BAM! BAM!" Three knocks on the Duty Hut

door. Try to break your hand by knocking or be harassed for being a sissy whose hands are too soft to knock like a man.

"What is it, private?"

"Sir, Private Hann requests permission to enter the Duty Hut."

"Enter."

I marched into the Duty Hut and stood at attention before Sgt. Camp. He looked at me but I stared straight ahead, above him. Anyone who looked a DI in the eye would encounter the DI's wrath, expressed as, "Are you eyeballing me, private?"

"Sir! Private Hann requests permission to speak to the Drill Instructor."

"Speak."

"Sir, my foot locker doesn't have a shelf." Sgt. Camp motioned towards the recesses of the Duty Hut. Several shelves lay stacked up.

"Get one."

As I pulled a shelf from the pile Sgt. Camp said,

"You're about a squirrely-looking motherfucker, aren't you?"

That made me mad. I knew Sgt. Camp expected me to answer "Yes Sir." that I was a squirrely-looking mother-fucker. I did look squirrely for sure, maybe more than many of my fellow recruits because of my small, slim build and my eye glasses. I knew that, but at that moment I didn't care. I had been treated like a subhuman long enough.

"No Sir!"

Sgt. Camp did a double-take. When he drew back I thought he was going to hit me. Instead he said,

"Get your gear and get out. Straighten out your foot locker and report back to me."

"Aye Aye Sir." And I did and that is how I became the first House Mouse of Platoon 174. The second House

Mouse was Bastunas, a portly native of Sacramento who was overcome with heat exhaustion just a few hours later. Did I say it was hot in San Diego? The third House Mouse was DJ (Red) Constant, the Cajun from Thibodaux, Louisiana, whose bushy hair I had noticed. DIs selected him because he was the first recruit to respond to Bastunas when he collapsed from heat exhaustion. Also, I believe the DIs were intrigued by his Cajun accent.

Some Marines say that the House Mouse gets preferential treatment from Drill Instructors. That may have been the case in other platoons, but in 174 I was often singled out to go over obstacles first and, like my fellow House Mice, was occasionally harassed by Drill Instructors from my own platoon as well as the three other platoons in our series. Also, when the call "House Mouse" came we three had to drop whatever we were doing and rush to the Duty Hut. Whatever we were working on remained where it was until we finished whatever task the DIs had in mind. That meant if we were cleaning rifles I could expect my rifle to have a fine coat of dust and the same condition went for boots. Sometimes the voice from the Duty Hut would yell out "House Mouse Hann," and I would rush off to see what lay in store for me.

Over the next few days we met the other Drill Instructors, Corporal Miller, Sergeant Rine, and Platoon Gunnery Sergeant Berger. Cpl. Miller was a glowering Black man in his early twenties who radiated hostility towards us all, but especially towards the Black recruits. Sgt. Rine was a short, wiry man, full of dark humor. Sgt. Camp, the Senior Drill Instructor, was a Mormon, which I thought strange to find in the Marine Corps, and he had his own brand of dark humor. Gunnery Sergeant Berger stood at least 6'2" and must have weighed a solid 230 lbs.

I was the first person hit by Corporal Miller. The dry

California air made me susceptible to nose bleeds. Corporal Miller entered the Quonset hut and someone called "Attention!"

We stood stiffly at attention. Corporal Miller stalked past me. My nose began to bleed and I instinctively brought my hand up to stop the bleeding. Corporal Miller wheeled around and punched me in the stomach, knocking the wind out of me.

"You will stand at attention in the presence of a Drill Instructor Private Hann. Do you understand me?"

"Yes Sir," I croaked, barely able to speak.

"I can't hear you!"

"Sir, yes sir," I said using what air I had left.

"You're going to make a good little Marine, aren't you Private?"

"Sir, yes sir."

Miller glided around our Quonset hut. Blood dribbled from my nose. I tried to quietly sniff the blood back. Finally Miller left to go lay down the law in the other Quonset huts of our platoon.

Miller hit a few more recruits as the days passed. Once, I was an indirect victim. I stood behind Private Young, a Black kid from California, needing to see Corporal Miller for some reason. Young must have not stood straight enough or done something else to annoy Miller, or maybe Miller just felt like hitting someone. He stood in the doorway to the Quonset hut, his hands grasping the ledge over the doorway.

Miller suddenly pulled himself up and kicked Young right in the stomach with both feet. That catapulted Young backwards into me but neither one of us went down.

"You will stand at attention Private Young."

"Yes Sir." At least Young hadn't had the wind knocked out of him. Later, Young told me he had crossed his hands in front of his groin, otherwise Miller may have done him some damage. The backs of Young's hands were red where Miller's boots had struck.

Miller sent Young off and I stepped up. Miller regarded me with his hateful gaze. A fly landed on my forehead and crawled over my eye. I instinctively closed my eye.

"Are you winking at me, private?"

"No sir."

"You leave that fly alone, private. He don't eat much."

Whatever my purpose in being there I forget now, but I remembered the lesson of my nosebleed and stood stiffly as the fly crawled over my face. The fly crawled across my lip and lingered at the edges before coming to my nose. My lips and nose tickled like mad but I kept my face rigid, eyes straight ahead. Miller asked me some questions and my answer startled the fly and he took off. Miller dismissed me and I took off too. Recruits never walked anywhere unless we were marching. All other times we ran. Recruits double-timed or ran wherever they went, sometimes with slung rifles, sometimes with rifles, packs, and helmets, sometimes wearing nothing other than our utilities.

In addition to countless pushups, side-straddle hops, squat thrusts, and running, we ran in place holding our rifles above our heads. Eventually one's arms could not hold up the rifle and it crashed down on our heads. Of course we continued running with the rifle bouncing up and down on our heads. We ran to all our classes, and ran to the Conditioning Course, Endurance Course, Physical Drill Under Arms, and Log Drill.

Our first day at Log Drill, Gunney Berger picked up a log meant for six recruits, hefted it up onto one shoulder then up and onto the other shoulder before throwing it down in disgust. "Bah! Dried out. Too light."

The Log Drill was an exercise with six to eight men

lifting one log depending on its size. The purpose of the log drill was that we learned to work in unison. If one man's grasp slipped he could endanger the rest. We lifted the log from the ground, transferred it to one shoulder then lifted and transferred it to the other shoulder. We even tossed the log up above our heads and caught it, which really required one's attention. We also lay on our backs and reached behind our heads to lift the log up and onto our chest, like a bench press.

"That's what 'Gung Ho' means, privates," explained Sgt. Rine as we struggled with the weight of the log, "working together." Sgt. Rine also used "Gung Ho" during our mass punishment exercises, when one recruit made a mistake of some kind, stressing that one man's mistake could endanger his fellow Marines.

On our first day of Log Drill, Pvt. Landry somehow inched backwards each time we lifted the log. When we set down the log it came down on Landry's face. He didn't sustain a broken nose or fracture bones in his face but when he returned from Sick Bay he looked really awful, his face swollen and bruised. Landry stuck it out though, exhibiting toughness we all aspired to.

The first time we went to the Conditioning Course Sgt. Camp called me:

"Pvt. Hann, catch every recruit in that platoon ahead of us and stand at attention when you're finished. Get going."

"Aye Aye, Sir." I scrambled up the 30-foot tall triangle called The Tower, down the other side, ran along a horizontal beam, leapt off that, crawled through a corrugated metal tunnel, stepped along the tops of a series of 3-foot posts, passing recruits from the first platoon all the way. The last two challenges were to run, leap to grab a rope, swing across a shallow water pit, climb up a rope cargo net and down the other side. I was surprised to see the recruit next to me slip off the rope into the water, much to the rage of his drill instructor. I swung safely across, scrambled up the cargo net, down the other side and stood to attention in our waiting area.

The other recruits in my platoon began to arrive, a couple looking like they had slipped off the rope into the water. I received no acknowledgement from Sgt. Camp but that didn't bother me. I preferred not to be noticed, as did every recruit in our platoon.

The first time I earned positive notice was our first physical fitness test. I scored second highest in our platoon. Sgt. Camp hadn't read the scores and names before calling us to attention. After giving us "At Ease" he began reading the scores. Private Padgette scored the highest with 328 out of a possible 400. I scored 316, earning a look of surprise from Sgt. Camp.

The second time I caught the DIs' attention was when I fell out of the three-mile run in our first Combat Readiness Test (CRT). For the CRT we wore helmet, pack, cartridge belt with two canteens of water, and cast iron rifle slung over the right shoulder. Wearing this gear I climbed a thirty foot rope to the top of a beam, slapped the beam and descended. Next I ran fifty yards, picked up another recruit and slung him over my shoulder in a "fireman's carry." I had to sling his rifle over my shoulder too. It was my bad luck to carry an overweight, stocky guy who weighed at least 150 lbs. I somehow picked him up and lugged him back to the starting point. All this was done running in sand, by the way, and the sand absorbed energy. The third test was running, diving to the sand, bringing up the rifle to shoot, then running and leaping over an eight-foot wide ditch. Pvt. Moore went first and badly misjudged the width. Moore leaped high but not far and down he went. Of course he had to do it again. Luckily for Moore, he had missed the beams running the width of the ditch, which was about five feet deep. Recruits had been injured by hitting the beams after failing to jump the ditch. Somehow I made it but Series Gunnery Sergeant Crawford didn't like that I went down on one knee after making the leap. I had to go around and do it again! Lucky for me I cleared the ditch again, this time to the satisfaction of the Series Gunny.

I had done all right so far but the last thing we did was the three-mile run, really a slow jog, but the equipment carried made this difficult, so difficult that eventually I dropped out. This was very, very bad. I think eight of us didn't make it.

When our platoon returned to the barracks Sgt. Camp took us failures to a dirt square, where we did pushups and squat thrusts until ready to drop. Of course all this was done while being described in the most unflattering terms by Sgt. Camp. Next day, while doing close order drill with rifles on the big cement parade ground called the grinder, Sgt. Camp and Sgt. Rine took me to task for falling out of the run. They were very displeased with me. After our platoon was called to halt, Sgt. Rine walked up behind me and spoke into my ear.

"There's Big Hann."

Sgt. Camp stepped in front of me and pulled my eyeglasses out until the strap was taut, then let it snap back onto my nose.

"Can't make a measly three miles."

"You best improve, private."

"Sir, yes sir."

Sgt. Rine and Sgt. Camp kept up this line of talk for awhile, Sgt. Camp snapping at my eyeglasses, Sgt. Rine making sarcastic comments in my ear, and then we were ordered to march. I expected, correctly, that more pushups lay ahead.

Corporal Miller was dismissed from our platoon just three weeks into our training. Miller had Private Petz doing pushups and Petz wasn't doing them to Miller's satisfaction. Miller kicked Petz in the head. After Miller dismissed Petz, Petz went to the duty hut and asked to speak to another Drill Instructor. Miller was absent then.

I heard Petz asking if Drill Instructors were allowed to kick recruits in the head. Petz was sent to Sick Bay to be checked for possible concussion. We didn't see Miller again until we marched to the Rifle Range at Camp Matthews.

The so-called "march" to the rifle range combined running with marching, including running up hills until legs could not function. Platoons marched in order of height, the taller recruits in front. This meant that the downward slope of hills allowed taller recruits an easy march down the hill while the "little end" had to run up the hill to keep the platoon closed up.

Even though the month was November the march alone made us hot and when we ran up hills we became hotter. Bastunas collapsed, sweat pouring from him, his utilities dark with perspiration. Sgt. Camp poured water over Bastunas's head. "Heat exhaustion."

We continued our march to the rifle range. It was just a few miles from the rifle range that we encountered a third battalion platoon. Because I was on the outside column of our platoon I could see that the third battalion platoon banner was that of my friends, Steve Kidwell and Mike Thoennes. Luck had it that both Thoennes and Kidwell marched on the outside column of their platoon and I marched on the outside column of my platoon. As our platoons passed one another I saw Kidwell and Thoennes. I took a big chance and called to each one by his last name. Each one saw me and grinned. Had I been caught communicating with recruits in another platoon I would have been punished by drill instructors from both platoons.

We lived in tents at the rifle range, tents with wood floors and frames, eight men to a tent. As we marched into the tent area we saw Corporal Miller standing, glowering, and to our delight he had one arm in a sling. Mixed with that delight was apprehension because we thought Cpl. Miller was coming back. But that was the last we saw of him. He never should have been chosen to be a Drill Instructor. Good riddance.

I had shot a fair amount as a teenager and considered myself a good shot. I assumed I would be an excellent shot with the M-14, but my teen shooting was just with my .22 caliber rifle shooting at objects less than 100 yards away. Shooting the .308 caliber M-14 rifle was a very different matter. The targets were much farther away, the rifle was heavier, the muzzle blast much louder and the recoil of the M-14 much stronger than the little .22 Marlin.

The minimum distance of a target at the Rifle Range was 200 yards. We had already become familiar with handling the M-14 in marching and in exercises. The 9.54 lb. M-14 began to feel heavy after a few minutes of running in place or holding the rifle straight out in front, parallel to the ground.

The first couple of days at the Rifle Range we spent Snapping In, where Marksmanship Instructors trained us how to hold and aim the rifle. You don't hold a rifle just any old way and the Marine Corps is very serious in seeing to it that every recruit practices the proper techniques. For example, in order to minimize recoil impact the rifle is pressed as tightly as possible into the shoulder. Recruits who didn't do so were rewarded with a bruised shoulder.

Every platoon was assigned a Preliminary Marksmanship Instructor (PMI) who oversaw our training. We were to qualify with our rifles by hitting targets in the standing, or "offhand" position, at 200 yards, sitting and kneeling at 300 yards, and prone at 500 yards. One hundred ninety points was the minimum to qualify, as Marksman. Two hundred ten points qualified as Sharpshooter, and two hundred-twenty points earned the highest qualification, Expert. By the way, I was left handed but that didn't matter. I was to qualify with the rifle by shooting right-handed, which also meant I had to use my right eye for sighting. That may be one reason why I did not do nearly as well as I assumed I would in my first live firing attempt.

One of the most difficult postures to assume was that of sitting because I had to cram the rifle into my shoulder. It felt like my rifle was too long to fit. While I was trying to cram the rifle into my shoulder the PMI, Sgt. Roberts, squatted down in front of me and chuckled at my discomfort.

"You look like a monkey playing with a stick, Private Hann. OK, Private Hann, take the rifle out."

I complied but the rifle was so tight it sprung from my shoulder and the muzzle clipped the PMI across his forehead.

"Ow!"

I expected the PMI would hit me but instead he said, "Why do you hate me, Pvt. Hann?"

"Sir, the private does not hate the PMI, sir!"

"Then why are you trying to kill me? Did you belong to some teenage gang back home?"

"Sir, no teenage gang, sir." I probably looked to be one of the least likely recruits in my platoon to belong to a teenage gang, however, this question was asked of me every now and then, I suppose appealing to some sense of humor.

I was very fortunate that the PMI was a patient, even kindly man, especially considering that he had enlisted at age 16 during the Korean War, bore a jagged scar on his left cheek, and had seen "bodies stacked like cordwood" during the Chosin Reservoir battle of the Korean War. PMI Sgt. Roberts worked with me until I could quickly and correctly assume the sitting position.

Our first stint firing at targets before Qualification Day did not please our DIs. Sgt. Camp halted us after we marched a mile or so from the shooting area.

"You privates think this is just a big game, don't you?"

"No Sir!"

"You buck and jerk and act like you're on some kind of vacation. You think this is some kind of holiday excursion?"

"No Sir!"

"Squat thrusts!" Sgt. Camp counted.

"One." We squatted down, hands on ground shoulder width.

"Two." We thrust our legs backwards, our arms held straight in what the DIs called the Leaning Rest position.

"Three." We brought our legs back to the squatting position, arms straight and hands on the ground.

"Four." We stood at attention.

"Twenty squat thrusts."

"Sir, twenty squat thrusts, Aye Aye Sir." And we began, counting the movements like so.

"One, two, three, four, one sir." And so on until we reached twenty.

We stood at attention huffing and puffing.

"On your backs." We quickly fell onto our backs.

"On your bellies." We quickly flipped over onto our bellies.

"On your backs. On your bellies." The orders came fast and we flipped back and forth several times before Sgt. Camp stopped us.

"Leaning rest position."

"Sir, Leaning Rest, Aye Aye Sir." We positioned ourselves on the hard ground, arms straight, hands shoulder width apart same as beginning pushups.

"Parade Rest." We crashed to the ground as we clapped our hands together behind our backs. Sgt. Camp repeated the Leaning Rest, Parade Rest combination several times before returning us to attention. Sgt. Camp had impressed us all with the seriousness of shooting.

Rifle training alternated with group exercises, mass punishment meted out to the entire platoon. In addition to Squat Thrusts, Pushups, Leaning Rest/Parade Rest we ran in place with our rifles over our heads, sometimes with our sea bags over our heads, marching on elbows and toes, and running, usually every day. I got to like the running without pack, rifle, canteens of water, and helmet.

The night before Qualification Day, or Qual Day, officially called Record Day, our DIs and the Series Gunnery Sergeant singled out those who had not yet shot a qualifying score. I was the first recruit called into the Duty Tent. Sgt. Camp, Platoon Gunnery Sergeant Berger, and Series Gunnery Sergeant Crawford were ready for me. Sgt. Camp sat on the edge of his bunk.

"On your knees Private Hann."

"Aye Aye Sir." I knelt down in front of Sgt. Camp. He held a pencil in one hand. Because I had been forced to shoot right handed I sometimes had trouble keeping my left eye closed. Sgt. Camp began tapping my left eye with the eraser end of the pencil.

"You're going to keep that left eye closed, aren't you Pvt. Hann?"

"Sir, Yes Sir." Sgt. Camp tapped my eye several more times.

"Elbows and toes." I assumed that position, holding my body off the floor of the tent, weight on elbows and tows, hands clasped behind my neck.

"Forward, march." I began marching on my elbows and toes while Sgt. Crawford sang the Marine Corps Hymn and Sgt. Camp counted cadence. Gunny Berger slipped off his wide Sam Brown belt and began to whip me on the ass.

"From the Halls of Montezuma..." "Whap!" "Owl eye owl eye."

"You're going to qualify tomorrow, aren't you Pvt. Hann?"

"Sir, yes sir."

"To the shores of Tripoli..." "Whap!" "Owl eye owl eye."

"You're going to shoot straight, aren't you Pvt. Hann?" "Whap."

"Yes Sir."

"We will fight our country's battles..." "Whap!" "Owl eye owl eye."

"You're going to keep that left eye closed, aren't you Pvt. Hann."

"Sir, yes sir."

"On the land as on the sea..." Gunnery Sgt. Crawford's voice boomed out loud enough to cover the sound of Gunnery Sgt. Berger's leather belt smacking me on my ass.

"Are you going to qualify tomorrow?"

"Yes sir."

"Are you going to qualify tomorrow?"

"Sir, yes sir."

"All right, get out." I got to my feet and got out, ass still stinging.

And so it went for an hour or so. Six of our platoons were called in and given the motivation treatment.

I awoke on Qual Day, to the familiar, "Platoon 174 on the road." Seventy-five voices responded, "SIR, PLATOON 174 ON THE ROAD, SIR."

We did a few front straddle hops to get loosened up, marched to chow and then marched to the Rifle Range. We had previously been assigned to places on the firing line and stood, waiting our turn.

PMI Roberts approached me while I waited and held forth a pill. "Here, take this, it'll help you relax." I don't know if the pill was a placebo or the real thing, but just that extra effort by the PMI made me feel better. I was determined to qualify. I don't recall my individual scores at the various distances of 200, 300, and 500 yards. I do recall PMI Roberts standing behind me on the 300 yard slow fire kneeling and rapid fire sitting positions. I did well in the rapid fire. I heard Sgt. Roberts say as one bull's eye after another was indicated for me. "Let it be, one more, let it be!"

Finally, at 500 yards I scored enough points for a total of 198, 8 points above the minimum. I made it, qualified! Marksman was the lowest level of shooting prowess but few other successes I have had were more meaningful.

We returned to our platoon tent area and stood at ease as Gunnery Sgt. Berger read our scores. He was surprisingly easy with the four recruits who had not qualified. They looked very dejected but Gunny Berger assured the non-quals they would have a chance to qualify when they got to their duty station. Nevertheless, for the next few weeks of our training our DIs selected the non-quals for particularly onerous tasks. Also, the DIs ordered the non-quals to run around our platoon on the march back to our regular barracks.

After Rifle Range, platoons in our series were assigned duties based on their overall scores academically, physical fitness test, close order drill, and rifle range. I believe our platoon ranked highest overall, including high shooting team at the Rifle Range, and so our duties were relatively easy, such as mowing lawns in the officer and staff non-commissioned officer areas, general cleaning, and occasional laundry detail.

The lowest ranking platoon was assigned mess duty,

demanding work that meant rising even earlier than our usual just-before dawn wake-up and working late into the evening.

Like all recruits I was always hungry and once had the good fortune to eat four meals in one day. I had been assigned laundry detail and upon returning to our platoon I found no one there. I assumed they had gone to evening chow so I double-timed to the chow hall and asked a DI with another platoon if I could join the chow line. I got my tray and quickly looked around for my platoon but they were not there. I hurriedly ate and then double-timed to our platoon area just in time to join them for chow. I relished that fourth meal but I was truly stuffed.

Fellow recruits Cusak and Constant had a good-natured rivalry over who would get the best score. Constant qualified as Marksman while Cusak qualified at the highest level, Expert. Bastunas, Constant, Cusak and I were in the same quonset hut. Our first night back from the range Cusak teased Constant right after we had retired to our bunks. We had been awarded our shooting badges and Cusak wore his Expert badge on his T-shirt so he could taunt Constant. "Where's your privy lid shooting badge?" asked Cusak, describing the square Marksmanship badge for which Constant qualified. Constant replied in Cajun, something uncomplimentary regarding Cusak's ancestry, I think.

As days progressed through November the nights and even days got markedly cooler. One evening we were in our Quonset huts, shivering. We had not been issued field jackets so all we had for warmth was our utility shirts worn over T-shirts. Sgt. Rine came into our hut and after we were called to attention he strode up to Pvt. Bugg, a Black recruit from Topeka.

"Stop that shivering, Pvt. Bugg."

"Sir, yes sir."

"You're still shivering, Pvt. Bugg. Stop that right now."

"Sir, the private cannot stop shivering."

"Well, private, get over next to that stove."

"Sir, the stove isn't lit."

"I know that, private. Use your imagination."

Before we left for our only night in the field Sgt. Camp called me into the duty hut. He handed me a sheet of paper.

"Memorize this quickly and report back to me."

I memorized the proclamation poem or whatever it should be called and returned to Sgt. Camp. The next morning Sgt. Camp called me into the duty hut and ordered me to shout the poem in front of each of the three Platoon 174 Quonset huts. I was embarrassed but gave it all I had.

"Sir! I'm lean and mean and weigh nine hundred pounds. I can lick my weight in tigers, lions, and bears. There is no one who can put me to shame for some have tried and I've gained my fame. Fighting, fucking, and wild bull riding is my game!"

Our night in the field was called "grab ass" by our DIs but that didn't mean they had gotten soft. Once we got to our camping area and assembled, another platoon marched up. Their DI said he was going to march his platoon right over ours. This infuriated Gunny Berger, who happened to be standing next to the other DI. Gunny Berger grabbed him by the back of his neck. "What are you going to do, turd?"

Gunny Berger shook the six-foot tall offending DI like he was a rag doll.

"What are you going to do?"

Releasing his grip, our Gunny spoke softly into the DI's ear. The DI gave his platoon the order to about face and marched away into the night. We swiftly set up our tents, careful not to say or do anything that might anger our Gunny. Once tents were up we ate C-rations, canned meals that we ate almost every day in the Infantry Training Regiment (ITR) that followed boot camp.

Next activity was called Commander's Time. Some of us were encouraged to perform skits or recite poems. I had already done my thing before so I was spared. Pvt. Billings sang a very amusing song to the tune of the popular hit, "Please Mr. Custer," which was about a cavalry soldier pleading with Gen. Custer not to go with him to the Little Big Horn.

"Please Mr. Berger, I don't want to go. There's a commie waiting out there, waiting to take my hair. Well, he's got his little carbine, and here I sit with my M-14..."

Then Cusak did something that influenced me for the rest of my life. He recited from memory Rudyard Kipling's *Ballad of East and West*, a very long poem. All of us, DIs included, were, I believe, surprised and impressed by his performance. After boot camp I learned that ballad and sixty years later can still recite it.

The last big test was the Combat Readiness Test (CRT). I have described what it entailed: loaded down with field pack, rifle, helmet, cartridge belt, bayonet, and two canteens of water. I climbed the 30-foot rope, slapped the beam, and descended. Private Alveraz climbed the 30-foot rope but slipped and fell down, yelling in pain. I don't recall if he continued the CRT that day. I did, however, and ran fifty yards, picked up the "fallen casualty," Pvt. Bugg this time, not the fireplug-like Herzog, who had been dropped from our platoon. I ran back carrying Bugg while he shouted encouragement to me, ran through sand to leap the 8-foot ditch, and then joined the platoon for the final test— the three-mile run. That was a struggle but I made it. During the run, Constant grabbed one private who was about to drop out and, gripping him by his pack, moved him along with the platoon. We all made it. To say I was relieved and proud is an understatement.

In spite of our excellent physical condition recruits could still meet with injury or illness. At one formation Reeves clutched his chest, overcome with pain. A visit to Sick Bay confirmed he had pneumonia. Our final bayonet drill involved competition with another platoon. Pvt. Wren, one of the Wren twins in our platoon, suffered a dislocated shoulder. The competition involved pugil sticks, that looked like lengths of broom handle with padded ends. The pugil sticks were marked to indicate the bayonet end (red stripe) and the butt end (white).

When my turn came to face an opponent from the other platoon, I was a bit dismayed to see a growling six feet tall recruit. Sgt. Camp advised,

"Run up and stick him in the gut."

I did that, and if I had a bayonet instead of the padded end, I would have skewered him good and proper. As it was, the recruit shrugged off my stomach hit and brought his pugil stick down hard on my padded head piece. That knocked me to my knees, but I rose and we parried back and forth before our match was ended. My head piece was jammed down so tightly that I struggled to take it off.

One recruit hit another so hard with the butt end of his pugil stick that he knocked his helmet off. The stricken recruit looked a little dazed but recovered enough to retrieve his helmet and rejoin the conflict.

Our hand-to-hand combat instruction only included one day in which we were instructed in choking and throwing, defense against a knife-wielding attacker, and use of a baton as a weapon. Our unarmed combat instructor, a tall, rangy Black sergeant, explained how easy it was to crush a throat.

"I was at the beach the other day and saw some muscle man drain a can of beer and call to the watching girls, 'Watch this' then crushed the can with one hand. The girls were impressed. All I had was an ice cream cone so I yelled, 'Oh, girls, girls (raising his voice to sound feminine I guess), watch this.' I took a big bite of my ice cream cone and then crushed it with one hand." The sergeant squeezed his hand shut.

We laughed and the sergeant continued.

"If you can crush an ice cream cone," the sergeant glanced at the recruit standing next to him, "you can kill this man here." And at that moment he grabbed the recruit by the throat, not hard, but convincingly.

"Remember the ice cream cone." And we did.

* * *

November 23, 1963, just a few weeks before our graduation we assembled for close-order drill under arms on the big grinder, the large parade ground. We stood at ease, our rifles held at right side, waiting for orders to march. Gunny Berger emerged from the Duty Hut. Tears streamed down his face as he announced that President Kennedy had been shot and killed. Gunny Berger had seen plenty of men killed in World War II and Korea and had probably killed men too, but he was clearly moved by this tragedy. We returned to our Quonset Huts for an hour or so before resuming our training.

* * *

A few days prior to graduation we boarded trucks to take us to Camp Pendleton, where we met our Infantry Training Regiment (ITR) platoon commanders and company commander for A Company, called Liberty A, we learned later. We all were shocked to hear the ITR instructors call us Marines. Of course, that was great to hear. We had earned the title but knew we had more to learn and endure.

Sergeant Marshal, a big, black platoon commander who pronounced his name as "Sahgent Mahshall," spoke in a high pitched voice, warning us of what to expect. His helmet barely fit over his big head.

"When we go up into those hills, any Marine who doesn't keep up, I'm gonna make a example of him."

None of us wanted to be made an example of, but we were in excellent condition and felt confident we would do all right. We were "Gung Ho."

Graduation Day came. My aunt drove down from Los Angeles for my graduation and drove me to her house afterwards. I wore my graduation dress greens and didn't even take off my garrison cap while I rode up to Los Angeles. The next day I flew home, wearing my dress greens as a private in the Marine Corps, one of thousands who had stood on those yellow footprints. Infantry Training Regiment still lay ahead but I was confident I could do anything they asked of me.

Chapter 15

INFANTRY TRAINING REGIMENT

Back from Christmas leave after 13 weeks boot camp at San Diego Marine Corps Recruit Depot (MCRD), I and other graduates from boot camp gathered at Company A headquarters, early January 1964, where we were to undergo training at ITR (Infantry Training Regiment), Camp Pendleton, California. Now, decades after I was in the Marine Corps, the infantry training after boot camp is called MTB, or Military Training Battalion. Most of our NCOs and officers at that time were World War II or Korean veterans.

A sergeant, looking to be about 6'2" and 230 lbs. formed us into three platoons. "Alright, Marines, form up into columns of four, thirteen men to a column."

Marines? Being called Marines initially surprised us because in boot camp we were regarded as somewhat less than human, much less Marines. But here we were at the Infantry Training Regiment and eager to learn basic infantry tactics and weapons.

The sergeant continued. "Ah am Sahgent Mahshall (Sergeant Marshall) and Ah'm goin' to lead you Marines up and down these hills."

Sergeant Marshall made a sweeping gesture to the hills rising south of us. He wore utilities, like us and was so big his metal helmet barely fit over his head.

"Any Marine can't keep up, Ah'm gonna make a example outta him."

In spite of Sergeant Marshall's threat we weren't worried. We had completed thirteen weeks of rigorous training in boot camp and figured we could handle whatever ITR had in store for us.

In boot camp we trained with the M-14, a 44-inch, 9.54 lb. rifle, the most advanced infantry rifle at that time, 1963. Here at Camp Pendleton, January 1964, we were issued M-1's, also referred to as the Garand Rifle, after its designer, John C. Garand, a civilian engineer employed at the Springfield Armory, Springfield, Mass. The Garand was the first semiautomatic military rifle used as a standard combat shoulder weapon and was considered to have been the best infantry weapon of World War II and Korean War. The rifle was just a bit shorter and lighter than the M-14. I came to really like the M-1, probably because I used it so much at ITR.

We learned that Company A was nicknamed Liberty A, because the Commanding Officer (CO) regularly gave liberty to the ITR trainees. Liberty meant we could leave our compound and even the base if permitted, but could not stay overnight. Leave, which we did not have during our ITR training. refers to vacation, whereby Marines may travel off the base, go home or elsewhere for several days.

After morning chow, we would fall out for morning muster wearing leather boots, helmet, rifle, pack, and web belt that held a bayonet and two canteens of water and our M-1 slung over the right shoulder. The pack held a mess kit, extra socks, first aid kit, and C-rations if we had any. I believe that the "C" in C-rations stands for "canned" because everything we carried was canned, with offerings ranging from spaghetti and meatballs, a favorite along with beans and franks, pork loaf (ugh), to the most coveted items— pound cake and chocolate. We were surprised to discover that each box of C-rations included four cigarettes in small boxes that displayed the brand of smokes. The military discontinued issuing cigarettes with C-rations in 1975. Sometimes we were served hot meals prepared previously and heated for distribution to the troops. I think this only happened once, and we lined up with our mess kits open to receive whatever was offered.

We were hungry most of the time due to constant exercise from marching, route step, double-timing, field problems and the occasional mass punishment usually given in the form of side straddle hops or push-ups. We endured so much mass punishment in boot camp that the straddle hops and push-ups were no problem.

The mornings were cool, high thirties or low forties, but we never wore our field jackets because we would soon be marching or running up and down those Camp Pendleton hills and would warm up quickly. It was far better to be a little cold than to sweat and then cool off and catch cold or bronchitis or even pneumonia.

We attended some indoor classes, but most were outdoors, usually watching weapons demonstrated and then firing them—rifle grenade, hand grenade, rocket launcher (commonly called bazooka), machine gun, and flame thrower, which was scary to watch and even more scary to fire.

We had been instructed in the handling and destructive characteristics of the hand grenade and now was the time to throw one. I descended a ladder into the eight-foot deep pit that had just room enough for me and the instructor, a corporal. The grenade instructor was very tense. I thought,

"What a job!" Because I am left-handed I was to turn the grenade upside down before pulling the pin. We had been told not to pick up the grenade if we dropped it. The instructor topside had mimed reaching down and bumping heads together with a trainee.

"Just stand there. Your instructor will pick it up and get rid of it if it is armed, or hand it back to you if you haven't pulled the pin."

So the idea was to hurl the grenade over the edge of the pit and crouch down.

"Ready," said the corporal. I extended my arm down and to the side, looking up at the rim of the pit. I wondered later if anyone had bounced the grenade off the rim back into the pit.

"Throw!"

I hurled the grenade up and over the rim.

"Okay," said the corporal. "Get down, Hann". He chuckled softly, with relief I thought. He pointed to the ladder.

"Go."

I went and the corporal waited for the next nervous Marine to throw a grenade.

We learned various infantry tactics, like how to ambush a line of enemy with the fire team leader directing how the fire should be laid down on the enemy. A fire team at that time, January 1964, consisted of a fire team leader who was a rifleman, which I was, simply by accident of alphabet, an automatic rifleman, called a BARman, for the Browning Automatic Rifle (BAR), a light machine gun, an ABARman, or assistant BARman who carried extra ammunition for the BAR besides his own rifle. The fourth member of the fire team was a rifleman, who like the rest of us, carried an M-1. The BAR weighed just under twenty pounds and featured a bipod for using in sustained fire. We only used the BAR a few times, for which I believe the BARman was grateful, not having to carry that load.

These ambush exercises were "live fire" exercises. Our target was a line of 55 gallon drums 100 yards or so from our position, The usual directive given by the fire team leader was for him to aim at the front of the column, the BARman raking the length of the column, and the a-BARman and the fourth rifleman to aim at the rear of the column. It was important, at least in our training, to lay down coordinated directed fire to annihilate the enemy.

This is how we were trained although a goodly number of us, including me, wouldn't see combat, but we all received basic infantry training, just in case. Later, some of us, including me, would serve as riflemen in certain situations, such as riding guard on trucks (called riding shotgun), perimeter watch, or bunker watch. Marines slated for the infantry or "grunts," received much more rigorous training in ITR than we did in "Liberty A." One company was called Running Mike and that company consisted mainly of Marines headed for the grunts, where they would receive more rigorous and more intense training in infantry tactics and weapons.

We learned about house-to-house fighting, assaulting positions, how to react to an ambush, how to set up a defense perimeter. We alternated these practice assaults and defenses with more instruction on weapons.

The most awesome and scary weapon was the flamethrower. It held about ten gallons, 60 lb., of jellied gasoline. Each one of us was to slip on the flamethrower and trudge to the top of a low hill, one person at a time, and fire the thing. We had gotten used to wearing our 30-40 lb. packs, two canteens of water, helmet, and rifle, so the 60 lb. was just a bit more than usual. The first step, once reaching the top of the hill and sighting on the target, was to press the trigger just enough to activate the piezo ignition. The flamethrower nozzle spat out sparks. The next pull of the trigger caused the pressurized gasoline to spurt out of the tube and ignite just a few yards from the barrel. It was awesome, it was hot, and it was scary, firing at a rate of one-half gallon a second and enveloping the target in fire. Ten gallons of jellied gasoline gone in twenty seconds. The flamethrower pack was much lighter descending the hill, as was my rapidly beating heart.

The rocket launcher, or bazooka, was the most fun to shoot. The bazooka shoot was a two-man operation. The shooter shouldered the bazooka and the loader inserted the rocket into the bazooka tube. I sighted on the target while the rocket was inserted. Like the flame thrower, the rocket launcher was set off by a piezo ignition. The loader tapped me on the helmet to let me know I could shoot. The loader rolled away to the side, safe from the back blast. A WHOOSH and the rocket shot out, right on target, a rusted old tank. There was a satisfying BOOM as the rocket exploded. This was fun! Then it was my turn to load and roll to the side. I felt the heat of the back blast as the rocket shot forward.

One bit of training we all dreaded was the gas chamber. We all heard from others how unpleasant it would be. When the day came, I and my fellow Marines, hearts heavy with dread, tripped into the gas chamber wearing our gas masks. Once we were all inside and the tear gas was activated we had to take off our masks, put them on, and clear them by exhaling forcefully. A few breaths and we were breathing filtered air. The signal given, we trooped outside and removed our masks, eyes burning, noses streaming. It wasn't as bad as we expected.

ITR was fun compared to boot camp. Sure, we were tired most of the time, and hungry too, but once we had completed the day's work, whether it was a field problem house-to-house fighting, or assaulting a machine gun position or instruction on some weapon, we were own after evening chow unless we were conducting a night problem, which meant we had our C rations in the field. We never called our meals anything but chow, never breakfast or lunch or supper, but morning chow, noon chow, or evening chow. Sometimes, if we were in the field our chow was C rations, the same canned goods provided during WWII or the Korean War. A non-smoker could do well, trading cigarettes for coveted chocolate or pound cake that came with C rations.

Our field problems included firing blank ammunition or live rounds, depending on the assignment. The M-1 was a gas-operated semi-automatic rifle, which meant that a portion of the explosive charge that propelled the bullet bled off into a tube that ejected the shell casing, cocked the rifle and chambered the next round. The M-1 was loaded by pushing a charger clip of eight rounds into the open stationary clip. Firing blanks did not allow the M-1 to operate in semi-automatic mode and the rifle had to be cocked before each shot. With live rounds, the chamber ejected a round after the shot and when the last of the eight-round clip was fired the charger clip made a nice "ching" as the charger clip sprung from the rifle. I suggested to my fire team that we alternated shooting, so that someone was always firing while others cocked their weapons. That got a nod of approval from our platoon lieutenant.

Of course, against regulations, some ITR trainees kept back blank rounds. Such was the case one night, when after a day's field problem Schnitzer leaned out from his top bunk and yelled out, "So long, Nelson." Nelson looked back and Schnitzer fired. Nelson flinched of course and Schnitzer laughed maniacally. We all had developed a sort of dark humor from boot camp.

Discipline wasn't as harsh at ITR as it was in boot camp, but transgressors were punished. One trainee caught smoking when smoking was not permitted was made to light up his smoke and jog in place wearing a bucket over his head. When the offender was allowed to stop jogging, he lifted the bucket from his head and his eyes and nose watered and his face wore a tinge of green.

We shivered at morning muster, but we would soon be running these hills or striding along in route step. Route step? Imagine taking a long step and continue doing so until called to halt or double-time (i.e. jog). I was always able to keep up and even years later automatically fell into route step while walking. I guess daily training for one month accounted for that. The chilly weather and rigorous training, getting hot and sweaty route stepping up and down those Camp Pendleton hills caused many of us to get severe colds or bronchitis, even pneumonia. Toward the end of our time at ITR, our platoon of about forty trainees was whittled down to about twenty souls still ready and able to go. Showing a bit of uncharacteristic humor, Sgt. Marshall looked at our reduced number and instead of yelling "Platoon, Attention!" called the remnants of our platoon to order by barking, "Detail, attention!" Then we set off for that day's work.

One morning we were dismayed to discover the showers had no hot water. I don't know if losing warm water for showers was planned or not, but some of us braved the cold and took the cold showers, and quickly. I don't recall anything similar happening at other times at ITR so I am inclined to believe the loss of hot water was intentional.

M-1s were prone to jam with blank ammunition. During one field problem we were to attack in a line. My M-1 jammed and grabbing a rock I stopped and tried to hammer back the bolt. Our platoon lieutenant came up, grabbed my rifle, stood it on end and stomped back the bolt with his boot heel. "Now get back into that line!" he yelled. I was lucky to get away with only a verbal command.

While I was at ITR, Mike Thoennes, with whom I had enlisted, came to visit. Because I had been held back so I could get a waiver to enlist due to my poor vision. I didn't go through boot camp or ITR with Mike. He was departing for flight school and looked me up and came by to say hello. That was the last time I saw Mike. He became an A-4 pilot, providing close air support to Marines in Vietnam and was shot down and killed, Memorial Day, 1967, several months after I had left Vietnam and the Marine Corps.

The culminating exercise in our ITR training was a night problem. We were to defend a hill. After marching route step up the hill, we took our positions in prepared fighting holes. We were off duty on a Sunday, the day before our last field problem. I and fellow fire-team member, Horner, took a jaunt up a nearby hill called "Old Smokey." One would think we had enough hill climbing but it was great to get out on our own. As we roamed around, we discovered an ammunition carrier filled with M-1 blank cartridges, all in charger clips, which we shared with our fire team and squad. We would be able to really lay down the fire when the assault came.

It was cold and got colder when the sun went down. We had learned to load our clips into the M-1 without looking at them so we could keep our eyes on the terrain ahead. I loaded a clip into my rifle but quickly realized something didn't feel right. I removed the clip and saw that I had loaded live rounds into my rifle! Left over from a live-fire exercise earlier in the day. I was cold before but that really sent a chill up my spine. I took the clip of live rounds and buried it deep in my fighting hole, then stomped it down for good measure.

We waited, shivering, night fell dark and cold. Our squad had the blank rounds we had been issued for this exercise, plus the rounds that Horner and I had found and shared with our squad. I barely made out an image moving up the hill towards our position and thanked Providence that I had discovered the live rounds. I fired, and everyone, aggressors and defenders, opened up. Of course our squad continued to fire after the rest of the platoon ran out of ammunition. That was it, our last field problem.

We only had a few days left before exiting ITR. Sgt. Marshall had enjoyed haranguing us new Marines. "You never would have made it through the Chosin," he often yelled. He referred to the Battle of the Chosin Reservoir, an epic battle in subzero conditions during the Korean War, in which he and about 17,000 other Marines and some U.S. Army and some British Marines fought off about 110,000 Chinese soldiers. Sgt. Marshall insisted that we each give him a cigar for leading us through our training. I don't think I was the only Marine that inserted an exploding load into Sgt. Marshall's cigar. We were safely out of Camp Pendleton by the time Sgt. Marshall got around to enjoying his cigars.

Chapter 16

UNCERTAIN VOYAGE

August, 1965, one of thirty Marines from Electronic Maintenance Company, I stood in line with other members of the 300 or so 1st Force Service Battalion and looked up at the *Montrose*, Attack Transport (APA), that was to take us from San Diego to Okinawa. Baker, Kribley, Williams and I adjusted our pack straps, and, hands resting on our sea bags, waited for the order to board.

Baker said, "Scuttlebutt is that the *Montrose* has already sunk twice, once during World War II in the harbor at Long Beach and once during the Korean War in the harbor at San Diego."

"Third time's the charm," said Kribley. "Victory at sea," said Williams, recalling the popular World War II documentary.

The *Montrose* had carried Marines to beaches in the Pacific, battled kamikazes off Okinawa in World War II, and landed Marines in the Korean War. Now it was the Vietnam War, and the *Montrose* sat before us, her long gangplank ready to lead three hundred Marines onto the deck.

My field transport pack consisting of a knapsack and strapped below that a haversack, hung from my shoulders. A canvas tarp, called a shelter-half, lay over my pack, rolled and folded into a U-shaped cylinder. A steel helmet, secured with a strap, hugged my head. My M-14 rifle was slung over my right shoulder, my right hand grasping the sling. A wide canvas web belt with bayonet and two canteens of water weighed on my hips. The field transport pack clipped onto my web belt. We would appreciate having the two canteens of water handy because drinking fountains, or scuttlebutts, were scarce luxuries onboard The *Montrose*. The Navy and Marine term for rumor, "scuttlebutt," comes from the Navy name for drinking fountain, and the tendency of people to exchange gossip around such a gathering place became "scuttlebutt."

If a Marine fell into the drink, he was to unclasp the web belt, shrug off the pack, and claw to the surface. The free hand did the clawing, the other held the rifle. A Marine was never, ever, to lose his rifle. The knapsack held our mess kit, change of clothes, toilet articles, etc. In the field it would hold c-rations, letters from home, extra ammunition and whatever else we could think of. The haversack held an extra pair of boots and change of socks. My feet wore the other pair of boots.

I hoisted my sea bag onto my left shoulder and stepped onto the gangplank, my right hand gripping the rifle sling. I, as did the other Marines, carried all my possessions on my back.

"I packed too many books," I grunted.

"I stuffed a few of mine in your seabag when you weren't looking," said Kribley.

"Me too," said Williams.

I staggered up the gangplank with my fellow Marines and made my way down the narrow steps (called "ladders" in Navy and Marine parlance) into one of the lower decks of the *Montrose*. We stowed our gear and were allowed to make our way topside and watch as the *Montrose* slid out of San Diego harbor. Still within sight of land, two whales surfaced and swam alongside the ship.

Kribley whacked me on the shoulder. "A good omen."

Williams shook his head. "We'll need it." Williams was a poor swimmer and hated the idea of heading out onto the ocean.

At dusk we were ordered below. Our cots hung from chains, six cots, one slung below the other. We locked our sea bags and rifles to the chains. When the ship rolled the cots swung and, eventually, we Marines were rocked to sleep on our first night at sea. The *Montrose* joined other ships in a convoy and headed toward the North Pacific with Okinawa our destination.

In the weeks that came we read, we played various card games, Monopoly, and Parcheesi. We dozed in our cots or found a shady place on deck and napped; we got short-tempered from the boredom and fought one another. Each day Williams and I gazed over the ship's side into the ocean. We saw jellyfish, fishing net floats, and a lot of water.

"You know what that is?" Williams would ask.

"That's the Pacific Ocean," was my standard answer.

"That's instant death," was the standard answer from the non-swimming Williams.

Our platoon commander, fearing that we would get out-of-shape, had Sergeant Bill Slaughter organize physical training. The aptly-named Sgt. Slaughter had earned a brown belt in karate and put us all through exercises he used for karate conditioning. As much as we grumbled we knew it was doing us some good. Baker also did me a good turn by insisting that I apologize to Sgt. Slaughter for complaining so much about getting my head shaved prior to shipping out. I hadn't wanted to be bald for my last date with my girlfriend.

"Sgt. Slaughter?" I said as I approached the legendary

former brawler and practitioner of karate.

He turned his basilisk gaze on me, his eyes glittering like brown flint. Try to imagine dark granite chiseled into the shape of a man who moved with the fluid power of a panther.

"What is it, Hann?"

"I want to apologize for being such an ass about my haircut," I said.

Sgt. Slaughter regarded me, the flint gradually softened. "That's all right, Hann."

Later, on Okinawa, Baker got me to practice karate at the same dojo as Sgt. Slaughter. It was then I understood how really foolish I had been in my behavior. The thumpings and bruises I received by sparring with Sgt. Slaughter were nothing compared to what he could do if he was angry.

The *Montrose* and the group it sailed with turned north. The days became cool, and then became cold as our ship plowed through the North Pacific. The daily exercises warmed us and broke up our boring routine and then, something happened to change things before the added exercises became boring.

One night, the hatch to our area banged open and sailors dashed down the ladder to the deck below ours.

"They've got fire extinguishers," noted Kribley.

The next day, when we were allowed topside, we noticed the other ships.

"Hey," said Kribley, "why are they turning away from us?" "They aren't turning away from us," said Williams, "We're turning away from them."

Actually, the *Montrose* wasn't turning so much as it was drifting away. The fire down below had damaged the steering control. The seas became rougher, and the *Montrose* drifted into a storm from which the other ships were able to avoid.

Even though the seas were rough, some of us liked to ride the heaving deck on the fantail, the rearmost part of the ship. We hung over the edge and watched the propellers lift out of the sea and rattle. This happened whenever the *Montrose* buried her nose in the sea, about every 30 seconds it seemed. That lifted the stern so high that the ship's propeller left the water. (Years later I learned that the sudden strain induced on the freely rotating propeller shaft when it plunged into the sea sometimes snapped the shaft. Without power to the propeller, the ship would have been truly helpless, and so would we.)

"Ride 'em cowboy!" whooped Kribley as the propeller crashed down into the waves.

"Ride, ride, ride the wild surf," we chorused, emulating a popular surfing song of the day.

Finally, the seas became so rough that the sailors told us to get below.

"Staff Sergeant Johnson's got it bad," said Baker. "Don't let the motion get to you, because it won't stop until we make landfall."

Some Marines did get seasick, but I was able to conquer my stomach's first impulse to succumb to nausea caused by the constant rolling and pitching of the *Montrose*.

I was also fortunate that my good friend, Baker, was an electronics genius and could fix anything through which electric current flowed. Baker quickly made friends with sailors who worked in the radio shack and who serviced radios and other electronics components on board the *Montrose*. Because of this, Baker had the run of the ship, and had access even to the bridge, where only designated *Montrose* officers and crew were allowed.

At sea, most Marines were not allowed topside at night, nor were we, but that didn't hinder Baker at all. Baker was always "squared away," in appearance and had qualified

with the M-14 as Expert, which was the highest rifle qualification category, but he had scant regard for rules. Baker
took me aside and inspected my appearance, having me
button a jacket pocket here, see that my brass belt buckle
was properly burnished, olive drab utilities neatly bloused
over my boots.

"Come on, Hann," urged Baker. "Let's get out of here
for awhile. The fresh air will do us good."

"Sounds good to me," I said.

Baker carefully savored this authorized trespass in the
guise of technical aid. We went to the bridge at night because we were certain to be stopped from our shipboard
roaming during daylight. The rough seas kept most people
below decks anyway, day or night. Of course, if challenged
Baker had a ready-made explanation, which was sometimes
true, that he was needed to help check out the electronics
equipment for the sailors.

"Lance Corporal Baker and Pfc. Hann," announced
Baker, "We're here to check the radar settings" or whatever
explanation seemed most plausible.

When we made our way to the bridge no one ques-
tioned why we were there. We felt the ocean spray splashed
up to bridge level when the bow of the *Montrose* plunged
into the sea. It felt great. One of the deck officers said, "You
two Marines don't seem to mind this weather very much."

"No, Sir," said Baker. "It's an honor to be here, Sir." And
he meant it.

Probably because our progress was slowed by the steering problem and the storm, we had to ration water for the
last week of transport. That meant cold, salt-water showers.
Nobody complained much. After all, that was a small part
of what Marines are expected to endure. If you couldn't
stomach a little cold water you had no business in the Marine Corps.

"Now we are salty Marines," said Kribley, referring to the sensation of feeling a film of salt on the skin after one of the salt water showers.

"Now I know what they really mean by the expression," "Old Salt," said Williams.

Eventually, the *Montrose* crew repaired the steering, turned away from the storm, and after 22 days at sea we arrived at Okinawa. Perhaps the docks were too crowded for us to exit the ship via a gangplank or maybe this was a good excuse to practice a beach landing. For whatever reason, we Marines exited the ship in the traditional way, with a beach landing. We climbed down a cargo net hung over the side into waiting landing craft, called Mike boats. Some sailors had fun throwing fireworks from the bow as we climbed down the cargo net.

We wore our field transport packs and carried everything else except our sea bags, which would be shipped to us at our new duty station, Electronics Maintenance Company, 3rd Force Service Regiment, 3rd Marine Division. Because of the bulkiness of the field transport pack, and because we had to use both hands to climb down the cargo net, our rifles had to be unslung, the sling then being knotted by the Marine behind so that the rifle hung diagonally over the whole pack. Once we arrived ashore the rifle could be unslung again and carried in the traditional sling arms over the shoulder.

"I heard on a ship's radio that the typhoon followed us to Okinawa," said Baker.

"Welcome to an island paradise," said Fatty Dave, a Marine from our company who had voyaged to Okinawa a few months before us.

We made it to our squad bay (something like a Spartan dormitory), just as word came to batten down for the storm. Within minutes of picking out our racks, or bunks, we were pushing our metal lockers against the windows to protect ourselves from flying glass in case the high winds threw debris through the windows. The wind blew hard, but the storm didn't reach our area with any real force. We heard that the storm struck a more northern part of Okinawa and did some heavy damage.

Unfortunately, some of us, including myself, had taken too well to the opportunities for boozing and partying. I was saved by my friend Baker, who decided that he had to change his way of life before he became a confirmed alcoholic.

"You should come to the dojo and practice karate with Sgt. Slaughter and me," said Baker. You and I both have been doing way too much boozing."

"Yeah," I said, "When do we start?"

"I've started already. You start tonight." And so, I began practicing karate that night and almost every evening thereafter until I went to Vietnam. I never advanced beyond the beginner's rank of white belt, but it was good exercise. Baker and Slaughter were even impressed by my losing performance in a contest with another dojo. The young Okinawan man was more skilled but I was more aggressive and so kept him off balance until he settled the contest by leaping up and lightly kicking me in the chest. He could have easily knocked me several feet, but the rule in that contest was to pull your punches.

One of the Marines who practiced karate at our dojo became very proficient in that martial art and had been admired by our taciturn, hard-bitten sensei (teacher). I saw his photo posted on a wall at the dojo.

"Who is that?" I asked Baker.

"Jensen. "He was the best student here, but that didn't help him in Vietnam. He was shot and killed within two weeks of getting in country. The sensei posted his photograph to honor him."

"Well, I hope our pictures don't end up being posted here."

"You said that right."

On Okinawa our Electronics Maintenance Company was located next to Motor Transport Company and we occasionally wandered over to look at some of the vehicles that had come back from Vietnam. We had already seen plenty of radios that reminded us there was a war on. Some radios had been pierced with bullets and shrapnel and were blood-stained. We had a pretty good idea of what had happened to the radio operators.

One Motor Transport Company truck in particular got our attention. The truck had hit a mine and the metal floor board on the passenger side was ripped open as though a giant fist had punched its way up through the floor board—a fist of fire and steel. We all thanked our luck at not having been assigned to Motor Transport. We didn't know that in a few months, in Vietnam, some of us would become very familiar with motor transport, sitting on the passenger side, riding shotgun.

Chapter 17

GETTING TO VIETNAM

The first thing I should say is that I was never in a fire fight and saw no combat other than seeing tracers in the hills and watching South Vietnam Air Force Skyraiders strafe soldiers of the Army of the Republic of South Vietnam (ARVN) during the Buddhist rebellion in 1966. The only artillery fire encountered was that of outgoing shells, nightly shot over our tents when I was stationed near Phu Bai.

We landed on Okinawa in September. A few months later, some of our company, including Baker, went to Vietnam. We learned that some of them had been assigned to patrol, perimeter guard, and shotgun (riding guard on trucks).

We knew that our radio repair M.O.S. (military occupational specialty) was always subject to change to that of rifleman. I imagine that most former Marines can tell you that the number 0300, (which we pronounced "oh three hundred") means rifleman. That is why, following boot camp, all Marines received one month's infantry training and why our company, since it was part of Force Service Regiment, required everyone to go through annual infantry training so that we had some chance of survival should we be called upon to be riflemen. Our company, like all

Marine companies, required its enlisted men to pass the Physical Readiness Test every three months. That involved a three-mile run, climbing a 30-foot rope, leaping over an 8-foot ditch, running 50 yards, hoisting another Marine into a "fireman's carry" and running back to the starting point. All of this activity was done wearing a helmet, rifle, pack, and carrying two canteens of water. Most of us in our company had lifted weights and run the hills around Camp Pendleton in order to stay in shape.

A few months after Baker and others had sailed to Vietnam, the *Talladega*, an attack transport, like The *Montrose*, carried me and several other Marines from our company to Vietnam. The voyage only took four days, each day hotter than the last as we approached Vietnam. Every day, machine gunners practiced their skills by shooting from the fantail at floating targets, a reminder of where we were going.

I had learned the importance of speaking at least a little of the language of a country while on Okinawa. Because I intended to go to Vietnam, I found a Vietnamese language course being offered by the Army. I spent hours studying and practicing and took the class again when I found there was no advanced class. I knew that we could be assigned to patrol or ride shotgun, and that might lead to a situation where a little knowledge of Vietnamese could be helpful.

I remembered to travel light this time, and even though I still wore the field transport pack, my sea bag was much lighter than when I had carried it aboard The *Montrose*. The *Talladega* arrived off the coast of Vietnam after four days and hung up on a sand bar near the Marine base at Chu Lai. The big swells off Chu Lai constantly shifted the sand bars so it wasn't possible to predict their location. One thing was sure, we were stuck. Perhaps that is why we once again exited the ship in the time proven Marine way, climbing down a cargo net into Mike boats.

As before, we wore field transport packs. As before, the Marine in back of me tied the sling so that it could be worn over the pack. We lined up by fire teams, that is, four men, with the second and third fire teams of that squad following so that we would be assembled by squad in the Mike boat. I and three other Marines were first in line to go over the side and climb down the cargo net. The heavy swells off-shore rolled the *Talladega* side to side.

The waiting Mike boat alternately banged against the side of the ship and then rolled off several yards before repeating the cycle. Each time the ship rolled away from the Mike boat it slammed the cargo net against the side of The *Talladega*. The four of us climbing down gripped the net tightly as the grey bulk of The *Talladega* rolled and slammed us against the side. The *Talladega* rolled the other way, and we swung over the sea between the Mike boat and ship. The Mike boat coxswain maneuvered to keep the net in the boat. I had only climbed down a few feet when the knot on my rifle sling slipped.

The Marine in back of me had not properly tied my rifle sling. I felt the tautness of the sling loosen and from the corner of my eye saw the end of the sling slip through the metal ring of my rifle. I grabbed the rifle with my right hand. There was no question of letting my rifle fall, either to sink in the sea or break on the deck of the Mike boat. A Marine doesn't lose his rifle. That was drummed, drilled, and beaten into us so that holding onto my rifle was automatic. That left me with the problem of how to get down the cargo net. I only had one hand free, so I had to let loose completely, drop down, and grab the cargo net with my left hand while my right hand gripped the rifle.

This worked twice. Then the rolling ship bumped me off the cargo net as I dropped down and I fell backwards, still gripping my rifle, onto the deck of the landing craft. I guess I dropped at least ten feet, and landed on my back. My field transport pack and helmet cushioned my fall but the impact stunned me and I was knocked out for a few seconds.

When I opened my eyes, I saw the Marines who had started down with me struggling to hold the cargo net in the landing craft. I leapt to the cargo net and grabbed hold. We clung to the net while the heavy swells forced the Mike boat away from the *Talladega*. We strained to hold the landing craft against the ship with our legs. Each time the swells brought the Mike boat in we slammed into the side of the ship.

The Marines following climbed over us into the landing craft and joined us, keeping the net from slipping over the side of the landing craft. Finally, the landing craft was full enough for us to release our hold on the cargo net and the Mike boat churned through the waves into shore. This was what the Marines called an unopposed landing; one in which no one was shooting at us.

We stayed just one night at Chu Lai, but I did find Baker, who true to form was well-established with an air-conditioned repair van. The van had to be air conditioned because of the sensitivity of the particular equipment he worked on.

"Welcome to Vietnam," said Baker. And he offered Stewart and me a shot of scotch.

"What's it like here?" asked Stewart.

"About the same as Okinawa, except that we don't have close order drill on Friday mornings, and we don't get liberty either."

"So, what's this we hear about patrols and so forth?" I asked.

"Oh, we get sent out sometimes, but the Corps spent

too much money training us to fix radios to risk losing us in the bush. Our patrols don't stray very far from the perimeter. I heard that you're likely to catch shotgun in Da Nang."

A few scotches later, Stewart and I ambled to our tent, made from our two shelter-halves. Next morning was a little rugged, due to the whiskey.

"I'm glad I cleaned my rifle as soon as we set up our tent."

"Yeah, when you didn't get up right away after falling into the Mike boat we thought maybe you broke your back."

"Nope, just stunned me, but my rifle was lying in a puddle of salt water when I picked it up."

Early in the morning we repacked our gear and boarded a Landing Ship Dock (LSD) that took us to Da Nang. The LSD looked like a micro-aircraft carrier in that it had a flat deck with almost no superstructure. I suppose helicopters could have landed on the deck. The ship had a large ramp that dropped down onto the beach like a drawbridge.

I stood on the deck next to Gunnery Sergeant Sullivan. Gunny Sullivan said, "Are you going to stay out of trouble over here?"

"Yes sir."

"Well, the worst that can happen is they take you out and shoot you. Everything else is gravy."

"All right," ordered Gunny Sullivan, "Get into the hold and load our sea bags into the truck. You better take a good swig from your canteen before setting to it. It's 120 degrees in there."

"Aye aye Gunny," we replied, and scrambled into the hold. We labored for thirty minutes or so, heaving sea bags to Marines in the truck who wrestled them into place. Our olive drab utilities turned dark green from the sweat. We sat on top of our sea bags for the long ride to our company quarters. We saw our first Vietnamese soldiers, part of a long line of trucks carrying men and equipment.

"They don't look very humble, do they?"

"They fought the French for decades and the Chinese for hundreds of years. They've got nothing to be humble about."

Hours later we stood in the dirt rectangle of 3rd Force Service Regiment's mustering area, surrounded by the wooden-floored tents we were to live in during our stay in Vietnam. Luxury compared to shipboard quarters and beyond comparison to what the infantry had.

The company commander greeted us after giving the at ease command.

"The uniform of the day is cartridge belt, rifle, and utilities with shirt sleeves rolled up past the elbow."

We rolled up our shirt sleeves and immediately felt the sun burning our forearms. Okinawa had been cool, with temperatures in the 50s during the day.

"The temperature right now is 116 degrees," said the C.O. "Be sure and drink plenty of water."

The day had been long and we just had time to go to the mess hall for the evening meal. It was dark when we returned to our tents. Six of us were assigned to each tent. One of our group was Fender. Fender was an obnoxious sort who frequently boasted about how tough he was. Fender was just warming up, talking about how he could kick any Viet Cong's ass, when a voice broke into his talk.

"Is there a Fender in there?"

"Yeah," Fender yelled back. "What do you want?"

"You've got shotgun, Fender," the voice replied. "Get your rifle and helmet and flak jacket and get over to the motor pool."

"Wha…What?" queried Fender.

"Shotgun!" responded the voice, "Get a move on."

Noonan started it. "Say, Fender," asked Noonan. "What size are your boots?"

"Why the hell do you need to know?"

"Just in case something happens. You know…"

Then Nelson said, "You don't need to take your watch with you. Why don't you leave that here?"

"That's a good point," I said. "You aren't taking your camera, are you?"

And so it went. "What size are your utilities (olive-drab trousers)?" "How about your skivvies (underwear)?" We were merciless. Fender scooped up all his belongings and stuffed them into his sea bag.

"I'm not leaving anything for you bastards." And he stomped out of the tent.

Several hours later, in the wee hours of the morning, Fender stomped back into the tent. In behavior that was typical for Fender, he made no effort to be quiet as he entered the tent.

Noonan asked, "So, how was it?"

"Boring." Fender threw down his flak jacket and helmet and, giving us all a dark look, removed his boots and secured his rifle.

"Well," said Nelson, "Welcome back."

"F…k you guys," replied Fender.

"No sense of humor," said Noonan.

Chapter 18

DISPUTE IN DANANG 1966

All Marines are riflemen, or 0300s. 0311s were infantry, or grunts. So even though our main duty was to fix radios I, and others in Electronics Maintenance Company, 3rd Force Service Regiment, Vietnam, also served as bunker watch, perimeter guard, and guard on trucks, or shotgun. My first turn at shotgun came a few days after we landed in Da Nang.

Take off your flak jacket and get comfortable," the driver, Ryan, said. "Besides, we are more likely to hit a mine than to be ambushed during the day. I removed my bulky flak jacket and set it on the cab floor beneath my feet.

"That is definitely more comfortable," I agreed.

"Might save your legs if we hit a mine, too," said Ryan.

My first shotgun assignment was riding with a truck carrying concertina wire from the dock to a supply depot. We drove through the barren tidal flats and entered a scattering of one-story houses. We passed through the residential area and into the sprawling Marine supply depot. The smell of fresh asphalt and freshly-cut lumber floated in the humid air. Asphalt roads would keep roads navigable when the rains began in the fall. Dirt roads would become quagmires. Ryan piloted our truck through the near-chaos of vehicles and material as helicopters passed overhead.

One thing that I learned right away was how cumbersome the 44-inch long M-14 rifle was inside a truck cab. I had to avoid whacking the driver with the stock or the barrel while swinging the rifle into a firing position. The length of the M-14 and the narrow range of fire imposed by the truck window frame reduced the practical fire coverage area. Also, in our infantry training, we had never been taught how to fight from trucks.

In the weeks that followed many of us rode shotgun on supply trucks. Sometimes we were assigned trucks carrying cargo that by itself was not dangerous, such as concertina wire, soap, and c-rations. Other times we rode with ammunition and explosives, risky even back in The World, which is how we often referred to the United States.

Riding shotgun and the sometimes boring everyday routine of repairing radios, bunker watch, and perimeter guard became more exciting in April and May, when Vietnamese forces loyal to Premier Ky, a nominal Catholic, clashed with Vietnamese forces loyal to Lt. Gen. Nguyen Chanh Thi, a Bhuddist. General Thi commanded troops in in the "I Corps," the northernmost region of South Vietnam, where Marines made up most of the American troops.

South Vietnamese troops posted a mounted machine gun and trained it on our company's compound, just a hundred yards across a concertina-wire barrier and mine field. Someone higher up in the Marines ordered a recoilless rifle set up and pointed toward the machine gun. A recoilless rifle could fire explosive shells or antipersonnel loads, either of which would obliterate the machine gun and its crew. The back blast from the recoilless rifle, however, would take out some of our tents but the thirty-caliber machine gun manned by the Vietnamese could rake our entire company area.

The conflict between the Vietnamese factions continued with us Marines sitting right in the middle. One day in May we were rousted out before dawn and ordered to take up fighting positions a few hundred yards east of our company quarters. We settled into ready-made one- or two-man foxholes. Looking east, about one-half mile or so away, we could see Vietnamese Air Force Skyraiders diving to strafe enemy positions. The enemy was not the Viet Cong nor was it North Vietnamese Army, but South Vietnamese troops loyal to Premier Ky. Vapor spurted from wings of the diving planes first then we heard the rapid brrrap of the Skyraider machine guns. Marine Phantom jets circled above the Vietnamese Skyraiders. They were to shoot down any Vietnamese Skyraiders that headed toward our position.

"Well," said Nonan, "This is crazy."

"Yeah," I said, "I wonder whose side the Skyraiders are on."

"And who the hell they are shooting at," said Nelson.

The sun rose a little further through the scattered clouds. Philips, a heavy set Marine with a round, cherubic, though unshaven, face stood alone in a foxhole, his hands folded and resting on the earth in front of him. Other Marines stood in various postures, their rifles leaning against the side of their holes or slung from their shoulders. Suddenly several Marines burst out laughing.

"Look at Philips," someone yelled.

The sun had broken through the clouds and cast a sunbeam right on Philips. It was such an incongruous sight, Philips, with his helmet, flak jacket and rifle and the sunbeam spotlighting him like a religious postcard. I couldn't help but laugh with the rest.

The strafing continued for two hours, and then the Vietnamese planes and the Marine Phantom jets returned to base. We stayed in our foxholes for another hour or so then were ordered back to our quarters. Most Marines went to "the shop," our name for the area where we worked on radios. I was picked for shotgun. The driver, Forester, was to pick up bombs from a ship and transport them to the ammunition dump.

Forester drove a flatbed truck laden with bombs down a winding road with a few scattered houses and bushes along the road. It was another cloudless and hot day in Vietnam. I caught movement on the periphery of my vision, brought my rifle up, saw it was just a boy, and relaxed. Then the boy threw something under the truck. I didn't have time to shoot, which is just as well because nothing happened. We knew, however, that Viet Cong recruited children to throw explosives under trucks.

"God," I said, "I almost shot that little kid." Forester asked what happened and I told him.

"Probably was a grenade. Should have shot the little bastard," he said.

"What if it wasn't a grenade?" I asked.

"Then you'd be up for murdering a child," Forester said. "He probably didn't know to pull the pin. Anyway, we can't stop with this load of bombs to check out what it was."

I carefully scanned bushes we drove past, tense from what might have happened. We entered the city of Da Nang and drove through an area populated with some houses and other buildings. Forester and I both relaxed a bit. We stopped at a crossroads intersection. Facing us were half a dozen Vietnamese soldiers settled behind a bunker and their tripod-mounted machine gun. A metal fence barrier, mounted on wheels, blocked the road. Forester started swearing.

"Those, #%&# bastards. Don't' they know we're on the same side?"

Forester swung his door open and leaped out. He ran to the barrier and began to push it out of the way, swearing all the time. I don't know who was more shocked, the Vietnamese soldiers or me. Then I snapped out of my surprise and leapt out of the truck and began to help Forester. When we had finished pushing the barrier out of the way I remembered that I could speak Vietnamese, having taken a night class in that language while I was on Okinawa.

I said hello in Vietnamese to the Vietnamese soldiers. One of them said to his companions, "He speaks Vietnamese." I pointed towards the road we were to take. "We have to go straight." However, I used the collective pronoun for "we," "chung ta," instead of the exclusive pronoun, "chung toi." I had just told them that they and Forester and I all had to go straight, that is, we all had to go straight down the road. That really confused them. The soldiers looked at one another, puzzled. Then I realized what I had done and said again,

"We have to go straight" using the exclusive pronoun, meaning I was referring to Forester and me. The soldiers laughed then. One of them said "He said they have to go straight." The others repeated this, saying, di thang, or, go straight. They smiled and waved.

Forester stopped swearing and said, "What did you tell them?" I explained, including the information that at first they were confused because I had told them we all had to go down that road together. The Vietnamese soldiers waved some more.

Forester said, "Well I'll be damned." Just then, an American Air Force Military Policeman (MP) ran up to us.

"What do you think you're doing?" he said.

Forester said, "What does it look like we're doing? We're taking these damn bombs to the ammunition dump."

Air Force said, "You shouldn't have moved their roadblock. You could have caused an incident."

Forester said, "If you don't get out of my way there will be an incident of me kicking your ass."

"This is their country," said Air Force.

"That's right," I said, "and we're here helping them fight their war."

Forester and I turned our backs on the Air Force MP and resumed our journey to the ammunition dump. Thereafter, each time we came to the intersection the Vietnamese soldiers smiled and waved as they pushed the roadblock out of the way.

The situation settled down after a few days and I caught shotgun one more time before I got sent further north. This was riding shotgun at night, always scary. Different driver this time, Nichols, and instead of carrying bombs we carried rockets. Nichols watched the loading of pallets of rockets onto the truck bed. I kept an eye out for anything suspicious. After a few minutes several children began to gather. They didn't seem harmful to me so I ignored them until Nichols said I should make those kids keep their distance.

I pointed to a pallet of rockets swinging down from the ship onto the truck. "That can kill you," I told the kids in Vietnamese. The children's eyes widened, and they moved well away from the dock and the truck.

Nichols said, "What the hell did you tell them?" I explained and he nodded his head. "Good," he said.

The crane nestled the last load of rockets onto the flatbed truck and Nichols checked that the pallets of rockets were secure. We headed off into the darkness to the ammunition dump. A few miles from the loading dock we entered a dark and forbidding stretch of road.

"Truck got ambushed here a couple of days ago," said Nichols. He reached behind and up to the gunrack where his M-14 lay. With practiced smoothness Nichols plucked the rifle from the rack and set it down with the barrel resting on the dashboard.

"If we get hit," Nichols said, "shoot through the windshield." I swung my rifle up from between my legs and laid it across the dashboard too. I wondered about an ambush coming from the side but I figured Nichols's had the experience, so I followed his lead. I peered into the darkness but only saw blackness. There was no moonlight. Anyone could be waiting out there. We would only know that if someone opened fire on us.

We made several runs from the ship to the ammunition dump and had no trouble. I returned to my area around midnight. Rivulets of sweat ran down through the dust caked on my face and arms. I grabbed soap and towel and headed for our shower area. Since it was so late, I was not surprised to find that the water was gone.

I turned and started to return to my tent when a voice said, "Shotgun?"

I said, "Yes sir," and gesturing to the empty water tank added, "No water." I could see the speaker was a staff sergeant, meaning he was a noncommissioned officer. Showers were segregated among commissioned officers like lieutenants, noncommissioned officers, and lower-ranking enlisted men, like me, a lance corporal.

The staff sergeant said, "Go ahead and use this shower," and he pointed to the noncommissioned officers' shower.

"Thank you, sir," I said. The staff sergeant left and I hurriedly showered. I was just leaving the shower when another staff sergeant approached me.

"What are you doing in the noncommissioned officers' shower? You know that's not permitted."

"I know sir," I said. "Another staff sergeant said I could use the shower, since I just returned from shotgun."

"I don't care what you returned from," he said. "What's the name of the sergeant who gave you permission to use our shower?"

"I don't know his name," I said. I was pretty steamed at this pettiness. "And I wouldn't tell you if I did know his name."

"What's your name, Marine?" said the staff sergeant. I told him. The staff sergeant glared at me and stalked off. I returned to my tent. Two days later I was called into the company commander's office and informed that I and another Marine, Private Crabtree, were being sent to Phu Bai later that day.

"This isn't a punishment," the captain said. "Floozy Deuce (FLSU-2 or Force Logistic Support Unit Two) needs two more radio techs. Crabtree and I thought this was probably a punishment, but we were both glad to get out of Da Nang.

"So what did you do to earn this honor?" asked Crabtree. I explained and I asked Crabtree what he had done. "I cold cocked an obnoxious Corporal," he said. Crabtree was a little taller than six feet and probably weighed 180. I imagined he could knock someone out cold if he wanted to.

"I used to be Lance Corporal Crabtree," said the private. He had been busted down two ranks. "The only reason they didn't send me to the brig was that they actually do need me to fix radios."

Crabtree and I were the only passengers on the twin-engine DC-3 in its short flight over Hai Van Pass (Sea Cloud Pass) to Phu Bai. We flew low.

"Pretty country," I said.

"Except for the bomb and shell craters," pointed out Crabtree.

We traveled with several crates of electronic gear destined also for Phu Bai and touched down at the airstrip around noon. The pilot kept the engines running. The back-blast and exhaust from the big propellers added to the heat of the sun-baked landing field. The noise of the engines precluded talking, even shouting. Crabtree and I jumped down and stood ready to grab the crates as the loadmaster kicked them out. We reached up, grabbed a heavy crate, swung it down, and reached up again just in time to catch another. The crates were heavy, and the loadmaster was kicking them out of the plane as fast as he could. There was no enemy fire but maybe the pilot didn't want to be in such an exposed position, the only plane on the airstrip.

Next day my chest hurt so badly I went to the corpsman to see what was going on. Needles of pain forced me to take short, shallow breaths. I hadn't connected unloading the heavy gear with my chest pain, but the corpsman said the weight of the heavy crates had separated the cartilage around my chest on both sides.

"There's nothing to do about it," he said. "You don't want to wrap your chest because that could cause you to develop pneumonia. I could put you down for medivac."

"No thanks," I said. "I'd feel pretty bad getting medivacked for this when guys are getting shot and blown up. I can still do my job."

"Okay," said the corpsman, "I understand." My chest got better in a few weeks.

We were a very small unit of radio techs responsible for ensuring reliable communications for several battalions of Marines operating around Phu Bai and Hue. We worked on radios every day. Crabtree and I shared a small van and worked on the same type of electronic gear, a field telephone and a radio called a TRC 27 that allowed simultaneous communication among five different locations. Regimental and battalion commanders used the TRC 27 to talk with their battalions and companies.

Sometimes the generator that provided electricity to our shop conked out, stopping the tiny fan and raising the normal 105-degree repair van temperature to 115. Crabtree and I both swore at times when we got zapped by discharging capacitors or accidentally touched a hot connection. It was easy to be distracted in the heat with sweat dripping in our eyes and our uniforms draped onto our skins. Once a capacitor discharged direct current into my right arm through my chest into my left arm. My arms and my chest felt like they had been hammered with a club. We felt lucky to be fixing radios rather than slogging through the mud, rice paddies, and low hills. We could see tracers at night, and cannons fired over our tents often, the shells seeking an enemy we never saw.

Phu Bai was my last posting before I returned to the states. Thirty-six years later my wife, Rose, and I rode in a car over cloud-wrapped Hai Van pass and went through Phu Bai on our way to Hue. Our taxi passed over a bridge in Phu Bai, where as a young enlisted Marine of twenty-two, I used to walk over wearing a flak jacket and rifle.

Da Nang was my last experience with shotgun, or any kind of guard duty.

[Author's note: I only learned about the "big picture" details concerning the conflict between Premier Ky and General Thi much later. The Da Nang Project, by Terry Cochran, provides good background and his article references stories that appeared in Time magazine in April 1966. About 150 Vietnamese on both sides were killed in the fighting and another 700 were wounded. Twenty-three Americans, including eighteen Marines, were wounded.]

Chapter 19

BURY ME WITH MY FRIEND

A Memoir of Friendship in War and Beyond

I saw Linh's name on the return address, which had Irvine, California as her residence. That was when I knew that she was alive, that Linh had survived the war.

I had written to Linh's parents Hue, Vietnam, address in 1990, trying to find out if she was still alive, if her family was all right, and where my Vietnamese friends from 1966 were now. Linh explained that my letter came to her like a miracle. It had lain on her parents' table in their former home in Hue, Vietnam for more than two years, unopened. The last letter I had received from Linh was in 1975 just before U.S. military forces left the country and thousands of Vietnamese fled, were killed, or imprisoned.

Finally in 1993 I found out what happened. Linh explained that she and her family had escaped from Vietnam, but that Colonel Hau's plane had been shot down and lost in the jungle. Because of her education in the U.S., Linh's name was on a death list, but she and her sister escaped while mortar shells rained down around them. Linh's family home had been taken by another family. She didn't say what happened to her parents. When my wife Rose and I went to Vietnam in 2002 I phoned Linh and said I wanted to pay my respects to my old friend Col. Hau. Linh said that his plane was still lost in the jungle. We did visit and contributed a small amount to a school Linh was supporting near Hue.

After I retired from the University in 2009, I began to write, including some stories about my time in Vietnam. Then I recalled that I had saved all of Linh's correspondence to me, some twenty-one or so letters. As I read Linh's letters I was again impressed with Linh's dedication to help her fellow Vietnamese and her courage in returning to Vietnam while the war was raging. I felt that Linh's family should know about this aspect of her life and her thoughts at the time she was a young woman in a strange country musing over war, friendship, and duty.

My transcripts of Linh's letters take up about seventeen pages. I sent those to her, plus a digital copy of that file in the summer of 2012. Linh sent the digital file to Ky Lan, Hau's daughter who lives in Sweden. Linh's sister Luan never recovered from losing her beloved Hau. Ky Lan believed that sorrow and stress caused the cancer that killed her mother, but that Luan really died of grief.

Ky Lan emailed me expressing her gratitude for sending the transcripts to Linh and for my persistent friendship to her family. Ky Lan also said that she would not return to Vietnam because she did not like the communists who were responsible for her father's death and who had turned the country into a communist dictatorship. Linh feels the same way and had told me when Rose and I visited her and Van in Irvine in September 2012 that she knew if she returned to Vietnam, she would be unable to be silent about human rights and no doubt would be sent to prison there.

I had emailed Ky Lan in 2012 that Rose and I intended to go to Vietnam again, our having gone there two times before, in 2002 and in 2008. I remarked that I was sorry I could not pay my respects to her father. It was then that Ky Lan replied to me to say that her father's body had been recovered by a spiritualist, or shaman, who was able to contact Capt. Tru, Col. Hau's good friend and pilot of the plane shot down.

"Bury me with my friend." My Vietnamese friend, Yen, translated these words, spoken by the Abbess of a Buddhist orphanage south of Saigon. The Abbess explained how a shaman had contacted the spirit of pilot, Capt. Nguyen Binh Tru, who with his friend and mine, Colonel Nguyen Hau, had been shot down in 1975 in the waning days of the Vietnam War. Captain Tru said to the spiritualist, "I will help you find my body, but you must promise to also recover the body of my friend, Colonel Hau, and bury me with my friend."

I never forgot the kindness shown to me by Linh's family and struggled with conflicting emotions of wanting to find out what happened to them without getting them in trouble with the new rulers of Vietnam. In 1991, a Vietnamese student at the University of Kansas assured me that I could write without endangering my friends.

Although my main job in Vietnam was to fix radios, being Marines we were occasionally called upon to ride guard on trucks, that duty being described as "riding shotgun." If I had shotgun at night, I would not have to report for duty repairing radios until after noon. During that time, I would visit a Vietnamese family I had become friends with because I was a pen pal to a member of that family, Linh Tran, who attended the University of Ohio in Athens, Ohio.

I was a blue-collar kid from Kansas with one year of college and the last seven months of a three-year enlistment to be spent in Vietnam. I wanted to get to Vietnam and see what it was all about. Having been on Okinawa for several months, I had learned that speaking a little of the language of the country I was in made for better relations with its citizens. That is why I took a Vietnamese language class sponsored by the U.S. Army and that is how I had become friends with my pen pal at the University of Ohio.

Linh's brother Van was a fighter pilot and her brother-in-law Colonel Hau Nguyen was a wing commander, both of them being stationed in Da Nang, where I was until being sent farther north to Phu Bai. Van used to ride me on his motorcycle, him with his black silk flying suit and me with my green utilities (called fatigues in the Army) and M-14 rifle. Linh's sister Luan always fixed me something to eat, and Colonel Hau and I talked about many things. He advised me to finish college and remarked that knowledge of other languages would make me a citizen of the world. Hau could speak French, German, English, and a few Vietnamese dialects.

The Tran family and the Nguyen family had been highly educated, university people who lived in Hue but whom the war uprooted as it did thousands of Vietnamese.

When it came time for me to go to Phu Bai, Colonel Hau, Van, and Luan, along with Hau's and Luan's children - Hau and Ky Lan, gave me a swell going-away dinner. Neighbors of theirs waited on us and we had a wonderful time. After we finished our dinner and talked for awhile, Colonel Hau gave me a ride back to my compound in his jeep, with his two children riding in the back, giggling at my attempts to speak Vietnamese with them. I waved goodbye to them as they smiled and waved back. I never saw them again.

I tried to find the Nguyens and Van when I returned to Da Nang on my way back to the U.S. but they had moved. I only had the address of Linh's parents in Hue. I tried to visit them in Hue but they were living in what was then an unsecured area. I didn't mind risking myself, but I didn't want to put at risk my fellow Marine friends who some-how had wrangled a jeep and got themselves assigned as my bodyguards. So, I never met Linh's parents although I did have their address, sent to me by Linh in case I could see them.

I returned from Vietnam in September 1966 and vis-ited Linh in Athens, Ohio, a few weeks after I got to the states, or "The World", as we Marines referred to the U.S. I continued to correspond with Linh after she had returned to Vietnam until the fall of Vietnam in 1975. Then she stopped writing, why I didn't know.

I must digress here to explain that, in 2002, Rose and I had made friends with another Vietnamese student, one who came to my office seeking help with her research proj-ect. Yen (pronounced Yeen) became like a third daughter to us, visiting us often and entertaining us with her beau-tiful voice and guitar playing and her stories. It is Yen and her family who Rose and I have visited on our four trips to Vietnam. Yen was living in Saigon, now also referred to as Ho Chi Minh City although many South Vietnamese prefer the pre-communist takeover name of Saigon. Yen was building a program to help disabled people in Vietnam learn skills and find employment. The program, Disabili-ty Resource Development (DRD), is still ongoing, though administered by another Vietnamese now that Yen has re-tired. Yen and her sister and friends stay with Rose and I whenever they come to Lawrence. They are like family to us.

I determined to visit Colonel Hau's grave and pay my respects, no matter where in Vietnam it was. I forwarded to Yen the name of the Buddhist orphanage and shrine where Colonel Hau was buried. Yen found its location, just a few miles south of Saigon!

As always, Yen's sister Liang, a successful real estate en-trepreneur in Saigon, provided a car and driver for our visit.

Liang had accompanied Yen and another friend in 2008 when they had graciously taken us for a tour of the Mekong Delta.

We arrived in Ho Chi Minh City in March 2013, where our friend Yen and her family live, and drove to the orphanage. Yen translated for us while the Abbess of the Buddhist orphanage related what the spiritualist had told her of how Colonel Hau's plane and body had been found and recovered.

The spiritualist had contacted the spirit of the plane's pilot, Capt. Nguyen Binh Tru. There were only two people in the plane, the pilot and Colonel Hau. Captain Tru said to the spiritualist, "I will help you find my body, but you must promise to also recover the body of my friend, Colonel Hau, and bury me with my friend." The spiritualist agreed to do that and a search party found the wreckage. Markings on the plane confirmed it was the plane flown by Captain Tru. The bodies were taken to the Buddhist orphanage and buried side by side at the small cemetery there. The shrine had photos of Captain Tru and Colonel Hau, and their gravestones have their names and photos displayed.

It was just a short walk from the main building to the cemetery, where I found the two graves lying side by side. I burnt incense to both Captain Tru and Colonel Hau. I sent photos to Ky Lan and to Linh, and Ky Lan sent me several poems written by Colonel Hau along with her thanks for the photos.

The circle of friendship that had been broken by the war, my departure from Da Nang to Phu Bai and by Colonel Hau's death was complete once again.

PART IV - OTHER STORIES

Chapter 20

BAD PRESS

Iwaited in the vault, my office in a former bank building. I was working but I was waiting for Duke to come down the stairs with his shotgun, to shoot me.

My boss, Myrell, had called me the night before. "Someone from Quenemo called me," she said, her voice sounding concerned. "Duke is furious that you didn't hire him. He's saying that he's coming to the office tomorrow and shotgun you. You know he's got a temper."

"I heard about his temper. Thanks for calling."

"What are you going to do?"

"Come to work, like usual. You know it was the board's decision not to hire him for Handyman Supervisor," I said.

"Yes," said Myrell. "It's like shooting the messenger. And you were the messenger. You don't have to come in."

"No, I'll be there tomorrow."

The next morning, I drove from my home in Lawrence to the Franklin County Police Department in Ottawa before going to the office. I reported what Myrell had told me. The desk sergeant leaned back in his chair. "Did he threaten you personally?" When I replied that the information was second-hand, third-hand, actually, the sergeant said, "Hmmm. We can't act on hearsay. There's nothing we can do."

"I understand."

"If he threatens you personally, or waves a gun at you, let us know."

"Right," I said, wondering if the sergeant noted the sarcasm in my voice. I had expected such a reaction from the police, and for the first and only time in my life, since my time in the Marine Corps, took a weapon to work. When I returned to my car, I pulled the .38 Special from under the driver's seat and slid it into my belt, covering the revolver with my sweater and my jacket. I had the .38 because a few of my friends and I were avid handgun shooters.

We used to drive down by the Kansas River west of Merriam and shoot tin cans and bottles. I had quit hunting several years before, finding myself dismayed and a little ashamed at killing a rabbit with a shotgun. If I had to hunt to eat, it wouldn't have bothered me, but I did it just for sport and it felt a little like murder. I guess being in Vietnam a few years before had caused me to outgrow my boyhood's urge for hunting and shooting live things.

Not that I had killed anyone in Vietnam, though there were some scary incidents. Maybe some people don't believe it, but a very common concern among soldiers and marines was the risk of shooting an innocent civilian. Choosing not to shoot in a questionable situation was a gamble; one I had taken and won, choosing not to shoot a boy who threw something under the truck I rode in. The driver, Forester, had said at the time, "You should have shot the little bastard. It probably was a grenade he threw under us, just didn't know to pull the pin." That sort of thing did happen. As it was, the boy who threw something under our truck loaded with bombs lived and so did we.

Anyway, that war was behind me. The bank vault was a lot roomier than the cab of a truck, but I was practically just as much an easy target in the bank vault as when I had been sitting in the cab of a truck in Vietnam. While on Okinawa we saw a truck that hit a land mine. The explosion had ripped through and peeled back the floor on the passenger, or shotgun side. The driver and shotgun guard, if not killed outright, must have been pretty messed up.

My friends and I had congratulated ourselves on being assigned to repair radios instead of driving trucks, not realizing that in a few months some of us would be riding shotgun on trucks in Vietnam. This was in keeping with the Marine Corps creed of "every man a rifleman," where anyone, no matter their MOS, i.e. military occupational specialty, was expected to fill the rifleman role when needed. Our four weeks in Infantry Training Regiment after boot camp taught us how to use machine guns, rocket launchers, grenade launchers, explosives, assault and defend positions, conduct and react to ambushes, but no one had taught us how to fight from trucks. The 44-inch M14 rifle was an unhandy firearm inside the cab of a truck.

So, while we mainly fixed radios, several of us were assigned shotgun, and therefore waiting for something bad to happen wasn't new for me. What concerned me at the moment, was whether or not I would have to shoot Duke, someone I liked but who might be mentally ill enough to shoot me.

The office secretary was surprised to see me walk into the office. "Didn't you hear about Duke?"

I shrugged. "I've got my job to do, take care of people's homes."

"You're crazy," she said.

I said nothing and proceeded down the stairs to my office in the old bank building, the bank vault, with its door removed. The only way out of the office was through the doorway and up the stairs. And that was the way Duke would come, if he did come.

I opened the top right-hand drawer and slid in the .38, leaving the drawer open. When someone came down the stairs I would see their feet and legs first. Seeing boots and jeans meant I would move the .38 from the drawer to my lap. I thought about the first meeting, three months before, between Duke and myself. I was scheduling provision of storm windows and insulation for elderly residents of the five Kansas counties served by MidWarm, my employer.

Duke Manshoult was the only person to apply for the handyman position in Osage County. He showed up just a few minutes after the office opened. "Duke Manshoult," he said, and extended a calloused hand, which took my hand in a firm, brief shake. "I heard you're looking for a handyman in Osage County. I'd like to apply."

"Great," I said, and got out the application. "I'll just ask a few questions and we'll go from there." I had learned the application process went far quicker if I asked the questions and wrote the answers myself. My own handwriting, printing actually, wasn't great but at least I could read it.

While I asked Duke the required questions I looked him over. Six feet plus, boots, jeans, denim shirt, denim jacket, Duke looked like the heavy straight out of an old grade-B Western, stringy dark hair, rough lean face, wary eyes, a working man, one used to hard work, indoors or out. I guessed we were about the same age, thirty-something, and what would have been much to his surprise, of similar background.

My relatives were blue-collar people who earned their living with their hands and backs, as I had done most of my life. To Duke and people at MidWarm, however, their first impression of me was of a college-educated white guy. They didn't know my college education was aided by the G.I. Bill. They didn't know I was a Vietnam veteran. My experience had been that when people knew my veteran status, their reaction most often was dismissive hostility, guarded friendliness, or distance. We had a bad press, and I learned to never mention it.

I also hired two men who were recent inmates at the state prison, for murder I was told. Buster, tall and wiry, like a rodeo bronc rider, his blond hair streaked with gray and his friend, John, shorter, powerfully built with a shock of white hair, had formed the S.O.S. Insulation Company.

"Don't hire them," said our bookkeeper, Betsy. "You never can tell with that kind."

Actually, I had experience working with "that kind" at a Kansas City company, SEQUAL, that had hired several former inmates. One I worked closely with, Curly, had served time for murder. If Mr. North, SEQUAL's owner, was willing to give former inmates a chance at reform I was willing to work alongside them. After Buster and John had demonstrated their knowledge and prowess about weatherizing homes, I included them among the small insulation businesses I contracted with and they excelled in their work.

It would take a while, me working side-by-side with the crews I hired, to show them I was a lot closer to them than they thought. I guessed that college-educated white guys had bad press too, especially when it was known they came from that hotbed of liberalism, the University of Kansas.

Duke lived in Quenemo, the most notorious, slighted town in Osage County. Quenemo was known for bikers, brawlers, and a general suspicion of strangers. I figured anyone living in Quenemo had to be tough.

"Good thing you're doing the writing," he said. "My handwriting ain't too good."

"No problem with that," I said. "Doing a little carpentry and installing storm windows doesn't require much writing. Looks like you've got plenty of experience." At this, Duke looked a little uneasy. He might have thought that having several different jobs would look bad.

"Jack of all trades," he said.

"Just what I need," I said. "You've got tools and transportation?"

"Sure do, out in my truck."

"Great! When can you start?"

"Right away."

"Outstanding. Let's get you signed up for payroll."

Duke looked surprised. "You mean I'm hired? Just like that?"

"Yes," I said, "just like that. You came here right on time to apply, and you've got experience and tools. Let's get started."

Duke extended his hand again and enclosed mine in a strong clasp. "Much obliged, sir."

"Just call me David, or Dave, no sir and no Mr."

"Okay, Mr. er, Dave."

So after I got Duke set up for payroll I helped him load his truck with the materials for Osage County residents, which surprised him. He turned to me.

"You're a regular fellow, aren't you?"

"Guess I am."

"You better give me a paper or something so I can show I'm working for MidWarm," he said. "People around here may think I stole those things."

Duke went right to work, and soon I heard words of praise about him from the Osage County MidWarm representative and elderly residents of Osage County. Duke worked fast and hard installing storm windows, and also took care of infiltration problems, that is, adding weather stripping and door sweeps to block cold air from getting in, plus the dozen or so other little things that taken together meant comfort to our elderly clients. Now, when he checked into the office to pick up orders, I noticed his confident walk and proud demeanor. He was doing good work and knew it, and I told him so too. I mentioned this to the Interim Director of MidWarm, Bob Carson.

"Duke never had a chance," he said. "His father was a notorious rough-houser and drinker and general good-for-nothing. In these rural counties, these small towns, blood ties carry the community's prejudices with them. If you were born a Manshoult, or a Gillespie (another family I had heard disparaged) you were assumed to be as bad as the other men or women in that family, sometimes going back generations."

"Well, he's the best worker I've got."

"I know. I hear he's working up a storm, but don't be surprised if you hear people putting him down because of his family name."

"I don't understand why people do that."

"The notion of class isn't restricted to the so-called upper-classes. You'll find that some lower-income people are jealous when someone they looked down on shows signs of succeeding at something. They'd rather see Duke stumble, do something wrong, than see him succeed."

Bob paused and looked at me, the ordinarily good-natured round face set in a grimace. "The same goes for you, too. You're not one of their own."

Well, I knew that. Right after being hired we were called to attend the MidWarm board meeting. The Black chairman didn't like me being hired. He wanted a Black person hired and insisted I be fired immediately. The MidWarm Director who had hired me resigned on the spot, as did the other person who had been hired with me. She was to be the Weatherization Coordinator, overseeing installation of attic insulation and storm windows on low-income and elderly residents of the six-county MidWarm Community Action Agency.

I stayed on because no one was going to run me off my job before I even started and by default was put in charge of the weatherization program. Just by the way, the Black chairman and I became friends after he saw I was fair and worked hard.

I found out that Bob was right about the backbiting. He regularly received unsubstantiated complaints about me from the Lynn County Coordinator, over whom I had been chosen as Weatherization Coordinator. And I soon heard things about Duke. Slim Bishop, an Osage County board member of MidWarm took me aside with another Osage County board member, Webster Grove.

"You better watch out for Duke," said Bishop. "He's crazy," said Grove. He threw a hammer at the mayor just last year."

"He's the best worker I've got," I said. "He's helping a lot of older people in your county be warmer this winter."

"You'll see," Bishop said. "He's on his best behavior now. "Now, he drives his truck around," said Grove, "like he was somebody important." I didn't understand how someone could look important driving around a truck, but I felt it was useless to argue.

Both because I was a hands-on type of supervisor, and because I wanted to get to know the work crews and have them get to know me, I often worked alongside them when I visited a work site. One day it was just Duke and me at Mrs. O'Dell's house in Quenemo. Mrs. O'Dell was known to be slipping a little mentally. I was on a ladder, having carried up a storm window and was preparing to install it over the double-hung regular window when Mrs. O'Dell rushed out of her back door swinging a broom.

"You damn Peeping Tom!" She then began to push against my ladder. I was lucky that Duke was there.

"Now, now," Mrs. O'Dell, that is the MidWarm man,

come to put in your storm windows. Don't you remember talking to me about that?"

Mrs. O'Dell thought a bit and contritely said, "Oh, Duke, you're right. I plumb forgot." She glanced up at me on the ladder. "I'm sorry Mr. MidWarm."

"That's all right, Mrs. O'Dell," I said. "I'm happy to help out." After Mrs. O'Dell went inside, Duke had to go and stand on the other side of his truck so Mrs. O'Dell couldn't see him laughing. I accompanied him by his truck and we both laughed until tears came to our eyes.

Duke did so well, especially helping our elderly clients, that I was pleased when he applied for MidWarm handyman Supervisor. I looked at the other applicants and decided to hire Duke. I admired his desire to better himself. The board went against my decision. I argued that he deserved a chance, but board members all agreed that Duke had risen as high as he had a right to. They didn't say that exactly, but I could tell that is what they were really saying.

"He ought to be satisfied with what he's got."

"A lot of people would like to be doing what he's doing, and for the pay he's getting."

I pointed out that I hadn't heard from anyone else in the county who wanted the job, that Duke was punctual and hard-working, dependable and honest. The board refused to budge. "Keeping him in his place," I thought.

Duke slumped in the chair next to my desk when I told him the news. MidWarm had chosen someone else.

"I recommended hiring you," I said, "but the board wanted someone experienced working with contracts." I didn't tell Duke what else board members said.

"He's crazy! Duke threw a brick at a councilman one time." I reflected at the time without saying it that the councilman probably had it coming.

"He carries a shotgun in his truck," said another board

member, who seemed to have forgotten that virtually every pickup truck owner in Osage County carried a shotgun in his truck.

"He's got a temper," said the MidWarm board chairman. "No telling how he'd react if he was working on a client's home, and they didn't like his work."

"I set the poorest table in the county," said Duke, mouth set in a tight line, looking into my eyes. "Know what we had for dinner last night? Mush, and hot dogs. Mush!"

"I'm sorry, Duke, but you are still the handyman for Osage County. This was a very poor second place prize, temporary day labor instead of a salaried position which would mean not only more money, but much-needed nourishment of pride wounded by a lifetime of slights. Like me, and Buster and John, Duke had a bad press.

"Well," said Duke, rising from his chair, "We'll see." He stood, hitched his jeans up on his rangy body, adjusted his denim jacket, pulled down his feed grain cap and stalked out of my office, up the stairs and out the door.

Now as I waited for Duke I wondered if the shotgun threat was even true, given the backbiting I had been victim of and witness to, and the observations of Mr. Carson about family prejudice. Footsteps sounded on the stairs.

Looking up I saw boots and jeans descending the stairs. I sighed and slid the .38 from the drawer to my lap. I recognized the denim jacket as Duke's. I grasped the .38 in my right hand, hoping Duke wouldn't be carrying a shotgun. Then I would have less than a second to shoot or be shot.

Duke descended the stairs and stood in the doorway, no shotgun. I exhaled.

"Morning, Duke."

"Morning, Dave." Duke took an awkward step forward and extended his hand.

"I want you to know I don't have any hard feelings about

you. I know it was them peckerwoods on the board."

I released my hold on the .38 and held it by the barrel with my left hand below the desk as I stood and extended my hand. "Thanks, Duke," I said. "That means a lot to me. I've got plenty of work lined up for you."

"I'm ready." Duke turned to go, then turned and looked me over with some concern. "You don't look so good. Not feeling well?"

"I wasn't," I said. "I feel much better now."

While I waited for my heartbeat to slow down I reflected that the four of us, Duke, Buster, John, and myself, were all in this together. We all had bad press.

Chapter 21

BLACKIE AND ME

Wishing to avoid the occasional raucous environment of my Michigan Street abode in Lawrence, Kansas after I had surgery in the Spring of 1974, I rented the hired-man's cottage on the Widow Dunn's farm house, near Clinton Lake, five miles west of Lawrence. I had been laid off from my job at KU and was recuperating from tendon graft surgery with my left arm in a cast and sling and my right leg tender from where a strip of tendon had been sliced. The graft ran from the center of my left palm inside my index finger, secured with a button on my finger-tip. The button would drop off in time.

Friends at 345 helped me load the car with my scant belongings, plus a five-gallon water container because the hired man's cottage only had cistern water, drawn by a hand pump on the kitchen counter. That was okay for washing dishes and clothes, but not fit for drinking.

The cottage was small. The tiny kitchen had a chair and small table and an electric stove. A propane stove heated the modest living room. A floor lamp stood next to a rocking chair by the stove. A worn couch sat across the living room and just off the couch a doorway led into the small bedroom. The bed took up most of the space there, leaving just enough room at the end for a chest of drawers.

I moved out to the Widow Dunn's farm in March and the weather was still cold, with several inches of snow covering the ground. The propane stove heated the house nicely, for a few hours. Shortly after sunset I noticed the room getting colder, and, I was sitting next to the stove, reading by the lamp light. I touched the stove, gingerly at first because it had been hot to the touch. This time, however, the stove was only warm.

Outside, the wind blew and rattled the window frames. A few minutes earlier the window-rattling wind contrasting with the heat radiating from my stove just made my little cottage feel cozy. Now, with heat rapidly ebbing from the stove and the house, the cabin seemed less a cozy retreat and more like a lonely cabin on the prairie.

The hired man's cottage wasn't isolated, however; my friends, Steve and Peggy, lived in the Widow Dunn's farmhouse just a hundred yards away. I knew I would be welcome if things became too cold to bear, but I didn't want to come seeking refuge on my very first night in the country.

I got my flashlight and coat and ventured outside. The propane tank dial indicated that the tank was empty. The Widow Dunn had forgotten to have the propane tank refilled. I would call her in the morning, but I had to make it through the increasingly colder night. I knew I could just go to bed until dawn but that didn't appeal to me. Then I remembered the oven—the electric oven in the kitchen.

I turned on the oven to warm, grabbed a blanket and a book to read and a beer to sip while the oven heated up, and dragged the rocking chair in front of the stove. I only had one good arm and one good leg, so it took some time to get comfortably situated in front of the stove.

Twenty minutes later I opened the oven door, took off my slippers, and pulled out the lowest oven rack. Blessed warm air flowed from the oven and paraphrasing Robert

Service, instead of stuffing Sam McGee into the blazing coals, I slid my stocking covered feet onto the oven rack.

Warm and content, I read and sipped beer while listening to Mary McPartland's Piano Jazz program on the local public radio station. Several hours later I grew drowsy enough to shut off the oven and go to bed.

Next morning, I phoned the Widow Dunn, who apologized for the oversight and had the propane man come out to fill the tank. Once filled, the propane tank kept me warm, and I could sit by the stove, reading and listening to the radio and howling coyotes and patter of rabbits around the little house.

I strolled outdoors into the snow-covered yard and to the outhouse, for my little home had no indoor plumbing. I walked around the house and saw rabbit tracks, and coyote tracks too. I grew accustomed to and got to savor the coyote howls and patter of animals around the place.

A couple of weeks after I moved in, it was time for the surgeon who had repaired my severed tendon to check on my progress. I drove a faded green automatic-transmission 59 Plymouth, the model with the shark fins, given to me by an elderly relative who had stopped driving.

So even though I could only use one arm and one leg I had no problem driving into Kansas City to the KU Medical Center for my appointment. The good doctor pronounced his operation a success and removed my cast. He advised me to gently use my hand but to take it easy with my index finger. I resumed playing my old guitar, given to me by another uncle who used to play mandolin and guitar before arthritis ended his playing. I never learned to play very well but banged away every evening before leaning the guitar against the couch and going to bed.

I had also become interested in film-making, so as the weather warmed I set up my Super 8 movie camera on a tripod and began shooting sunsets every evening just out-side my screened-in-porch. It was during these warming days that I heard a swishing sound coming from inside the house. The sound wasn't constant, so it took a few days to trace the source of the swishing to the screened-in-porch, which had a door leading into the house as well as the door leading outside. One afternoon I decided to investigate the mysterious swishing.

A broken-down couch and folding chair occupied the porch. The swishing sound resumed. It came from beneath the couch, where a large plastic bag lay under its far end. The plastic bag was moving. Some part of my subconscious knew what made the swishing sound before I saw it— a long blacksnake that slithered back and forth, apparently trying to get out of the bag. I suppose the snake had slipped into the bag to hibernate and was unable to find its way out.

"Well, Blackie," I said. "You've got yourself into a fine mess."

I grabbed my Super 8 movie camera and filmed Black-ie as he writhed inside the bag. I then opened the screen door, intending to drag the plastic bag outside to the front yard and set Blackie free. I grabbed the plastic bag and he instantly struck at my hand. The plastic covering saved me from getting a nasty bite. I retrieved the broom from the kitchen, planning to sweep bag and snake out the open door.

Before I could do this, Blackie punched his head through the bag. Using the broom, I guided him out the open door with one hand holding the broom, and the other operating my movie camera as I filmed Blackie's exit. I stepped back a pace when I saw how long he was. Lord, it seemed to take a long time for him to pass through the doorway. I pulled the door shut and latched it. I realized I had been holding my breath during all this and let it go with a sigh of relief that perhaps Blackie felt also.

Later, after filming another sunset, I sat in the rocking chair by the window, lamp on, reading. I heard a scraping noise in back of me. Turning, I saw the long form of Blackie, stretched vertically across the window panes. He moved his head back and forth as if seeking an opening in the window. I chuckled. "Sorry, Blackie, it's outdoors for you." I figured that he just wanted to get back into the house and hunt mice, for I had found a few mouse droppings around. I didn't have any mousetraps, so Blackie would be doing me a favor, but I didn't want him slithering around indoors while I slept, or while I was awake either.

Blackie finally gave up scraping against the window panes and I read some more, then went to bed and quickly fell asleep. It was in the wee hours of the morning when, "Kaa Ring," went my guitar strings. I woke, wide awake instantly. I knew, just knew, what played my guitar strings. I turned my head to the left and saw Blackie. He was coiled on the couch arm, head raised as if studying the painting of rural Kansas hanging behind the couch. His tail dangled over the guitar strings.

I threw back the covers and Blackie darted under the couch. The television show, Wild Kingdom, had been a favorite of mine as I grew up in Kansas City. I had longed for the exciting life of Marlin Perkins and fantasized about adventures with dangerous wild animals. I remembered how Marlin Perkins went about catching snakes and decided to make my own snake-catcher. I had rope, so I tied a slip knot onto the broom handle. Next, I looped my rope over the handle to keep it from dangling and maybe touching and startling Blackie. That would have to do.

I slowly moved the couch out from the wall. There lay Blackie, looking nervous as I felt. He vibrated his tail, which surprised me. I've learned since that some snakes did that, not just rattlesnakes. I recalled that Perkins carefully guided the loop over the snake's head, then tightened the loop. I did the same with Blackie and he didn't like it. He coiled around the broom handle. Keeping the loop snugged tight around Blackie's neck, I carried snake and broom outside into my front yard.

I was going to turn loose Blackie in my front yard, but I thought about how easy it had been for him to get back into the house and how he had slithered through my living room and over my guitar, just a few feet from where I slept. Keeping the loop tight around Blackie's neck I carried him back into the house and got my car keys.

The automatic transmission allowed me to start the car and drive with one hand, so I didn't have to loosen my grip on the broom handle. While Blackie writhed and hissed, I steered the Plymouth out of the farmyard onto the road. I found what I was looking for in just a few minutes; a pull-off area into a field, where a farmer entered with his tractor.

I stopped the car and keeping the loop tight around the protesting Blackie, got out. I carried Blackie and broom several yards from the car into the field, loosened the loop, and laid snake and broom on the ground. Blackie wriggled free and shot off into the grass.

Blackie did not return, and I moved back to Lawrence to look for work, putting farther distance between myself and Blackie, happy not to see him again. I suppose he felt the same way.

Chapter 22

THE NOBLE LADIES

I was moved to write this short story after a 1860s newspaper ran a story about a rivalry between two German noblewomen over the affections of a dashing cavalry officer that culminated in a bloody brawl.

Baroness Mahtilde von Schendel stepped from her horse-drawn carriage into a gust of wind. She gasped in dismay at her hair all awry.

Frau Sybilla von Nordhausen quickly guided her inside.

"Oh, that wind!" said the baroness. I should not have gone out of doors. Oh, and my hairdresser, Frederich, has been laid low by the grippe." Baroness Mahtilde von Schendel wore her hair in the manner of the wife of the Dutch ambassador, now visiting in Berlin. Several society women had taken up her style—hair parted in the middle and ringed with dangling curls. A wind gust had tangled the tresses.

Frau Sybilla von Nordhausen patted the shoulder of her dear friend.

"Mahtilde, do not trouble yourself so. I shall command my hairdresser, Wilhem, to come and make everything all right."

Frau Sybilla called to a footman and instructed him to fetch Wilhem and have him come post haste to rescue the unfortunate baroness from her plight.

"Now then, my Mahtilde, let us take an apertif and relax. We have hours before our soiree."

"Oh, Sybilla, whenever have I had a friend such as this?"

Sybilla guided Mahtilde to a small parlor, well-lit by the afternoon sun, and bade her sit.

"Did not you come to my assistance when my coach broke down on the way to the Mayor's celebration? And have we not always cherished and helped one another since we both entered the social scene here in Berlin?"

"Indeed," replied Mahtilde, "that is true, and you are my truest, dearest friend."

And so the two friends continued their conversation in that vein and at last Wilhem arrived and worked his magic on the coiffure of the baroness. Sybilla extended her small hand mirror to Mahtilde.

"You must see for yourself how beautiful you look."

Mahtilde regarded herself. "In all modesty I must agree with you."

"Then let us have a schnapps and proceed to the party."

"Oh," said Mahtilde, "Perhaps I shouldn't. I think I am gaining a few pounds too many." While not plump, Mahtilde did carry a few extra pounds.

"Oh, nonsense," said Sybilla, "You fill out your dress very well."

Sybilla's carriage deposited the two noble ladies, fashionably late, at the Mayor's palatial residence. The orchestra played waltzes by Strauss. Military officers sported plumage like male birds, with form-fitting cavalry breeches, the dark trousers accentuating the broad shoulders and narrow waists of young officers. Light blue sashes contrasted with light grey or charcoal uniforms from which hung bright medals and gold neck pieces. Epaulets, resembling fancy gold-braided clothes brushes graced officers' shoulders. Younger officers wore mustaches. Only older officers and civilians had beards, perhaps disguising softening chin lines. Some officers carried their headgear, embellished with feathers, brass, or gold.

Women's gowns were cut and colored and shaped to show off curves, natural and contrived, of the beautiful women. Billowing shoulders of cloth enveloped upper arms in some gowns, others incorporated voluminous, floppy sleeves. Mahtilde and Sybilla wore the new styles, Mahtilde's dress conforming to her Rubenesque figure, while Sybilla's dress hung languidly on her slender frame.

"Now the ball is complete," said Count Von Hern, host of the gala. "The two most beautiful women in Berlin are here at last."

Count Von Hern turned to a handsome cavalry officer. "Captain Welch, may I present Baroness Mahtilde von Schendel and Frau Sybilla von Nordhausen."

"Charmed, I am sure," replied Captain Welch, clicking his heels. Both women extended their hands and the captain grasped that of Baroness Mahtilde first, bowed, released the hand then grasped that of Frau Sybilla. Frau Sybilla raised her hand as Captain Welch bent over it so that her hand was close to the captain's lips. The captain responded by kissing the proffered hand. Sybilla did not see the flash of annoyance, quickly extinguished, that blazed in Mahtilde's eyes.

The diplomatic captain clicked his heels again. "How fortunate I am to have made the acquaintance of two jewels of Berlin." He turned to Baroness Mahtilde. May I have the honor of the next dance?"

This time the flash of annoyance passed through the eyes of Sybilla. She could not control the flush that colored her beautiful face, however, and employed her fan, both to cool off and to hide the pink color that quickly faded.

The dashing cavalry officer basked in the admiration of the alluring ladies and made sure to spread his attention equally, not only between the two he had first met, but to the others who used flashing eyes and fluttering fans to attract attention while feigning disinterest.

"Look at them," said Mahtilde, referring to the would-be competitors. "So obvious."

"And so vain," said Sybilla, though her last disapproving glance was toward her friend.

"Well, let them try to win him over," said Mahtilde. "I am sure we stand out from the others." Mahtilde swept her gaze around the room, stopping to gesture with her fan at a rough-featured officer who on his left cheek wore the dueling scar that had become a trend among the gallant Prussian military. "He looks like the caveman sketch from Neander."

Remains of a race of cavemen had been found in the Neander Valley near Dusseldorf, just four years before, in 1856, and newspapers had drawn representations of those individuals, based on descriptions from scientists. The officer did have a heavy brow, pronounced jaw, and broad face, so unlike the handsome Captain Welch.

Sybilla laughed, "Our own Neanderthal. Do be nice to him if he asks you for a dance. He is a colonel, after all."

Mahtilde said that her dance card would be full should the ugly colonel have the gall to ask her. Sybilla suggested that the colonel could influence the career interests of their young captain for good or for ill, so it would be wise to be courteous to him. The two women spoke with their heads together and slightly turned so they did not see Captain Welch approach, arm in arm with the colonel. They stopped in front of the two ladies.

"Baroness Mahtilde von Schendel, Frau Sybilla von Nordhausen," said Captain Welch, "may I present Colonel Von Schnell, my commanding officer."

The colonel clicked his heels. The ladies recovered quickly and Mahtilde extended her hand. "Charmed," said the colonel, grasping her hand. He bowed, released the lady's hand and turned to Sybilla, who extended her hand, holding it low so that the ugly colonel would not be tempted to kiss it. The colonel raised Sybilla's hand to his lips and kissed it. Sybilla saw Mahtilde smirk.

Sybilla readily accepted the colonel's invitation to dance and saw Mahtilde smirk again, but Sybilla had a plan. While the two danced Sybilla informed the colonel that he had greatly disappointed Mahtilde, who long ago had confessed her adoration of older high-ranking cavalry officers, especially the colonel.

"She will be heartbroken if you do not press your suit. Mahtilde is so worried that another lady will steal you away."

Sybilla noted the colonel's widened eyes of interest and was not at all disappointed when at the dance's conclusion he promptly escorted Sybilla from the dance floor to where Captain Welch and Mahtilde were conversing.

"Dear Mahtilde," purred Sybilla, "here is our good colonel." The colonel bowed, clicked his heels, and held out his hand in invitation. "Allow me the honor of this dance," he said.

This time Mahtilde noted the smirk on Sybilla's lips as Colonel Von Schnell escorted the baroness and Captain Welch guided Mahtilde to the dance floor. Mahtilde also noted that Sybilla skillfully positioned herself so that Captain Welch's back was to her and the Colonel.

"We are alike, you and I," said the Colonel.

Mahtilde stifled a gasp and managed to say in a light-hearted way, "Why Colonel, how interesting. Why do you say that?

"Because," said the Colonel, more firmly grasping Mahtilde's ample waist," "we are people of substance, not like so many of the scarecrow women I see here."

As the evening progressed, friends of the two ladies noted that they no longer stood together when not dancing. Before the soiree ended Baroness Mahtilde had a footman summon her own carriage, rather than ride back with Frau Sybilla.

The two former friends, former because war between the two ladies had been declared implicitly, no longer attended social functions together. Mischievous or malicious gossip reached the ears of Baroness von Schendel that Frau von Nordhausen had described the titled baroness as "having a label, much like that on a package of sausage, which fits her physique."

The next encounter between the two ladies took place at the Royal Opera House, where took place a performance of Acis and Galatea a two-act pastoral opera by George Frideric Handel.

Sybilla had somehow acquired an invitation from Captain Welch, immaculate in his Royal Horse Guards uniform, with its narrow crimson front on black background that extended to the high collar. Gleaming brass buttons set off diagonal stripes of gold on the captain's sleeves.

Frau Sybilla made sure she encountered the baroness.

"Why Baroness," exclaimed Sybilla, "how fortunate you were able to come, after all."

"After all, what?" asked Cecilia.

"I suppose your skin condition has improved," suggested Sybilla.

"My skin condition? It seems that your teeth are bleeding, or is that your lipstick? You really should be more careful."

"We really must take our seats," said Captain Welch, sudden sweat appearing on his forehead. "Pardon me, dear Baroness." And he quickly guided Sybilla away, but not before Mahtilde heard Sybilla say, "How unfortunate is the poor girl, her skin and all."

What in the past were cordial weekly tête à tête conversations about affairs in their social set no longer took place. Friends and acquaintances of the two women noticed that the air became noticeably colder whenever Sybilla and Cecilia gained sight of one another.

A birthday party saw the hostilities grow more obvious. Sybilla stood talking with members of the party, wine glass in hand, when a bump from behind spilled the wine onto Sybilla's sleeves and skirt.

"Oh," apologized Mahtilde, "so sorry."

Hearing Mahtilde's voice Sybilla's face turned pink at first, then grew darker when Mahtilde said, "Oh, dear, was it me or your epilepsy?"

"What!?" said Sybilla.

"Or perhaps it was the drink," said Mahtilde. "I'm not surprised."

"Livestock should not be permitted indoors," said Sybilla. "But of course those with a peasant background should not be blamed."

"And I am sure you have experience with a peasant background," replied Mahtilde.

More social functions featured more angry scenes between the two women. Both women were concerned that their enmity would drive away Captain Welch. One day, Mahtilde's footman approached, letter in hand.

"A message from Frau Von Nordausen, Baroness," said the footman.

Mahtilde read, "She requests a final interview."

"Yes, Baroness?"

"She suggests that she and I cast dice for the officer's preference."

Mahtilde scribbled on the message and gave it to the footman.

"Let her come here," said Mahtilde, "and we will settle this."

Mahtilde's footman admitted Sybilla when she arrived the next morning, and guided her to a small table in Mahtilde's bedroom. Mahtilde had been occupied in cutting doily patterns from paper. She put down the scissors when Sybilla approached.

Mahtilde pointed to the empty chair opposite hers.

"Sit," she said.

Sybilla sat and produced a set of dice and said, "Let us have one toss each and the winner may decide what she will do."

Mahtilde said, "You have been such a pig. You know the captain wouldn't marry a girl of low breeding."

"Sausage girl," answered Sybilla. "That's what Captain Welch calls you. I guess that is because you look like a pig."

"Liar!"

"Sausage!" Sybilla gripped the dice, her knuckles turning white.

"Even if you won the dice toss," said Mahtilde, "the captain would never accept you. He wishes to move up in social standing, not down."

"Then he wouldn't be interested in a so-called Baroness," said Sybilla, whose low-born father purchased his baronet."

"I am sure," said Mahtilde, "that you can trace your ancestry right back to the Neander Valley. You and Colonel

Neander make a nice couple."

Sybilla flung the dice into Mahtilde's face, hitting her in the eye. Mahtilde blinked from the pain and slapped Sybilla with the back of her hand. Sybilla upended the table onto Mahtilde's lap and sprang for her. The horrified footman raced away for help.

Mahtilde tore out a lump of Sybilla's hair and struck at her face with the scissors. Sybilla turned her head exposing the side of her face and Mahtilde's sharp scissors severed Sybilla's right ear.

Sybilla screamed, pulled a pin from her hair, and swept it across Mahtilde's face, catching the baroness's right eye.

Both women were covering the bleeding parts of their faces but still lashing out at one another with feet when servants arrived. Two male valets and two ladies in waiting separated them. Two escorted Sybilla to her carriage while the other two attended to Mahtilde.

At the hearing of the case in the Court of First Instance at Schoneberg, near Berlin, Baroness von Schendel produced a neatly folded paper packet, from which she took a bunch of her adversary's hair, which she flourished before the judge as she boasted,

"I have had my revenge and have damaged her beauty."

The judge awarded the baroness $100 damages for loss of her eye. Perhaps Sybilla was able to have her ear re-attached or perhaps Baroness von Schendel had more influence at court than her non-titled former friend because the judge awarded no damages to Sybilla.

Captain Welch requested and was granted a transfer to a cavalry squadron stationed far from Berlin.

Chapter 23

BABYSITTING GAVITT

I can honestly say I don't have "a way" with babies. Friends and relatives have seen how my wife Rose can sooth the most recalcitrant baby, just by jiggling it about for several minutes. For some reason, they thought I had the same magic touch. I looked forward to a relaxing afternoon with my niece Gavitt, far better than enduring the hassle of Christmas shopping.

"Gavitt will love playing with you," said her mother, Belle. "You'll have no problem," said Gavitt's father, Dick. "Piece of cake," said Rose. "We won't be long," said Lucille, Rose's sister. Gavitt, just eight months old, being held by Belle, looked at me through dark, brown eyes, apprehensively I thought. "We just have a bit more shopping to do before Christmas," said Rose. "We won't be long."

Belle tousled Gavitt's wispy brown hair and set her on the carpet next to the Christmas tree. Fascinated by the blinking lights and glittering bulbs Gavitt did not notice the four adults quietly slip out the door. She sat gazing up at the tree and I lay on the carpet nearby, ready to head off grabs at tree decorations. Colorfully wrapped presents circled the tree. Gavitt pounded on some of them for awhile, accentuating each tiny fist impact with "Ah, ah." No doubt, she was having fun.

I should have thought to put some music on or at least turn on the radio because without the other adults around things were too quiet, too easy to slip doubt and fear into the quiet spaces. Gavitt quit pounding, held her head as if listening, questing for some sound. "Ah, ah?" She sat up and looked to either side. "Ah, ah?"

I tried to fill in the empty silence. "Hey, Merry Christmas! Ho, ho, ho!"

"Ho, ho," Gavitt mimicked. "Ho, ho." Then, "Ah, ah?"

"Let's look on this side," I suggested, crawling by her to the side of the tree. I pounded on another present. "Ah, ah," I said. Gavitt joined in right away, whaling away at another package. "Ah, ah, ah!" We pounded Christmas gifts together for a few minutes, me imitating Gavitt, she imitating me. I kept up a steady patter of nonsense words, sometimes slipping in real sentences, such as, "Do you know how many reindeer Santa has?" knowing that Gavitt didn't understand what I was saying but hoping to keep the silence of her mother's abandonment from being noticed.

Gavitt quit pounding and crawled around the circle of presents, then stopped, sat up, and looked around. "Ah, ah?" she said, looking a little worried I thought. "Ah, ah?" She made another circle of the tree and stopped.

"Don't worry," I soothed, "Your mama will be back soon." Big mistake, introducing the mama word. Gavitt knew the mama word. "Mama?" she said, her lower lip beginning to quiver. "Mama?"

"She'll be right back," I said. "Look at this." I tapped a shiny red bulb ornament. "Ah, ah," I said, and pointed to a shiny green ornament close to her.

"Ahh," said Gavitt, a triumphant tone in her voice as she reached towards the bulb. "Ah!" she said, happily, and whisked the bulb from its branch. Gavitt regarded the pretty thing for a few seconds, and threw it away with a backhand motion over her shoulder. "Ahh," she said in a throaty satisfied voice.

"Ohh!" I said, "Oh no, don't throw the bulbs." But of course, Gavitt didn't understand me. I scrambled for the bulb, which had landed on the carpet. I looked back at Gavitt and saw her grab another bulb. Another satisfied "Ahh!" and that bulb flew back over her shoulder. She was really enjoying this, and bounced up and down on her soft rump, gurgling with happiness. This was fun, fun for Gavitt.

As I retrieved the second bulb Gavitt scrambled around the far side of the Christmas tree, little hands and knees pounding the carpet. I scrambled after her. She was quick. I didn't know babies could move that fast. I intercepted her tiny hand as it reached for another low-hanging bulb. "Oh, let's leave that one alone," I suggested, and that suggestion didn't go over very well. "Ah!" she demanded. "Ahhh!"

I found a small, brightly-wrapped present with her name on it. "Guess who this is for?" I asked, and tapped the wrapping. Like a falcon striking a songbird, Gavitt's hand snatched the package from my hands. She used it to pound the other presents. "Ah, ah," she said. "That's better," I said, "isn't it?" Gavitt stopped pounding and looked at me and threw the present back over her shoulder. I've since learned that several babies love to play the throw and retrieve game.

I weighed the pros and cons of retrieving the present and leaving Gavitt free to go at the other presents and ornaments. In the seconds I took to locate and retrieve the thrown present Gavitt had used a larger present to heave herself up on her chubby legs. She grasped a branch in each hand and gave them a hearty shake. "Ah, ah. Ho, ho," she said in that throaty way of noting supreme satisfaction. The bulbs jingled and the lights shook. This was fun.

Damn, but she had a strong grip on the branches. While

I unwrapped one hand Gavitt vigorously shook the remaining branch in her grasp, now bouncing up and down on her springy legs. I had to maneuver myself between her body and the tree so that I could work on freeing the last branch. Trouble with doing that was that once I did that my back was to her, and Gavitt took off thumping around the tree on hands and knees, pausing to snatch off a bulb and throw it away, then she dove into the presents and flailed her arms to scatter them about, laughing, or whatever approximates laughing in babies.

Gavitt seized a present and ripped off some of the wrapping and stuffed it into her mouth. She didn't like the taste and spat out the chewed mess onto another present.

I lunged and grabbed her foot but Gavitt kept struggling until her tiny shoe slipped off. She liked that feeling and paused to pull off her other shoe and cast that one up into the branches of the Christmas tree. She looked up at it, gurgling happily. I paused for breath and recalled reading about the ancient Greek wrestler, Anteaus, who grew stronger whenever he was thrown to the ground. It seemed Gavitt was a kind of Anteaus, who grew stronger as she scrambled on the floor, and I grew weaker trying to keep up, let alone control her.

I sank down onto the floor on my back. I heard Gavitt scrabbling among the presents and pounding on them. I knew I had to rise and prevent her from hurting herself. What if she decided to chew on the Christmas tree light cord? Maybe it was premonition because when I opened my eyes, I saw Gavitt tugging on the Christmas tree light cord. You could tell she liked the jiggling motion of the colored lights. I wondered if the lights were hot to the touch. Best not to take the chance. I covered a light with my hand just before Gavitt's tiny fingers closed on it. Oh, yes, hot all right. Not too painful for me but maybe so for her. There were so many lights for her to go for, so many for me to protect, and the bulbs, too, were very tempting, as were the presents. I had to steer Gavitt away from the tree.

"Come on, Gavitt, look at this." I held up a jingling little bear toy and shook it. She exhorted a short, "Ah," meaning I thought, "Big deal, I know about that." "Ahhh," she turned away from me and took off again, aiming for a nice, juicy, red bulb.

I pulled her away from the Christmas tree and the presents. I saw three bulbs resting on the rug and several mangled presents lying scattered near the tree. Gavitt struggled to escape my grasp and held out her little arms towards the tree, opening and closing her hands. "Ahh!" she pleaded. "You can play with them when your mama returns," I said, immediately regretting saying the mama word.

"Mama? Mama? MAMA! MAMA!" The mama word mixed with wails of anguish. Gavitt flung back a hand and a sharp, little fingernail struck the corner of my right eye. I released my right arm from her to rub the scratch and Gavitt twisted away from me but I grabbed her left arm. She was lunging for the tree, screaming "MAMA," me holding onto her arm with one hand and rubbing my bleeding scratch with the other hand when the adults burst through the door.

"We heard Gavitt crying when we got out of the car," said Lucille. "Is she hurt?"

Belle rushed to Gavitt and picked her up. The wailing ceased and I sank to the floor on my back. My wife and in-laws surveyed the chaos. "You look like you've been through hell," said Dick. "Let me get you a beer."

"Yes," I said from my position on the floor, hands covering my face. "Please don't leave me alone with her again."

Thirty-three years later, after Gavitt had completed undergraduate studies at Harvard and had completed Medical School at Stanford and married I sent this story to her. She emailed back immediately after getting it and said my story about babysitting her arrived the same day her doctor informed her that she was going to have a baby.

Author's Notes

I didn't begin to write until I had transcribed some of my relatives stories of growing up in western Kansas, riding the rails around World War I, and some later ones set around World War II. After I had shared them with friends and family several of them suggested I write about some of my own adventures and misadventures. So here we are. Seven of the twenty-three stories have to do principally with travel. Two of the other sixteen describe travel by ship to Okinawa and Vietnam during my time in the Marines. Six were stories told to me by relatives and friends. Seven are based on my own experiences, including four concerning my time in the Marine Corps. One story, "The Noble Ladies," was inspired by a story I read in an 1860s newspaper. I hope you enjoyed them.

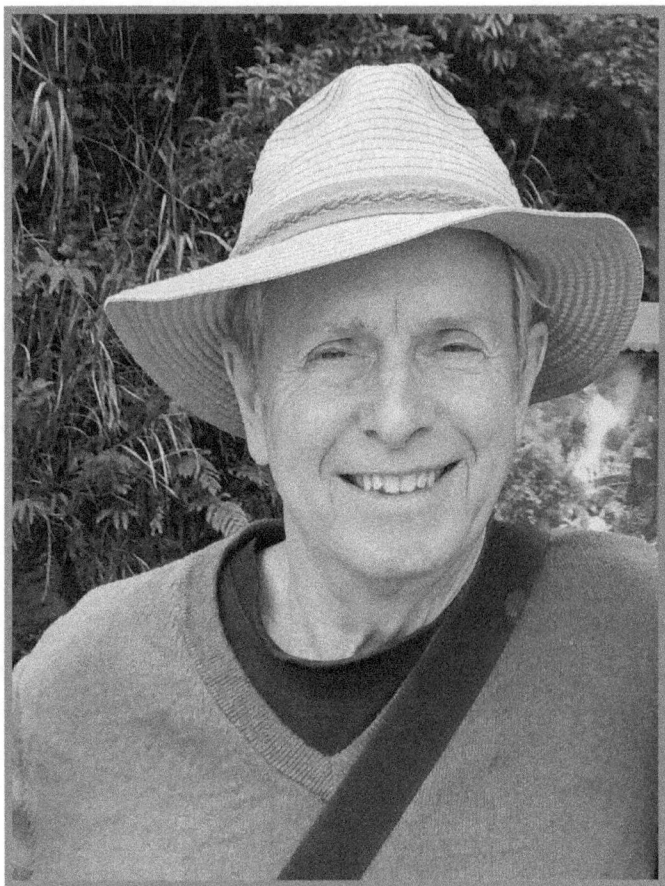

About The Author

DAVID HANN RETIRED FROM THE UNIVERSITY of Kansas in 2009, where he administered the university's Institutional Review Board. He is a Marine Corps veteran, Vietnam 1966. His interest in Kansas history prompted him to write two nonfiction books on little-known people, places, and events in Kansas, Sampling Kansas: A Guide to the Curious, and Kansas Past: Pieces of the 34th Star. Hann's interest in Kansas history led him to discover a remarkable character, Marshall Cleveland, from the Kansas/Missouri Border War years. Anamcara Press published Hann's story about him in The Jayhawker Cleveland: Phantom Horseman of the Prairie in November 2021. Other writings include a collection of short stories: River Memoir and other stories, and some poems, including The Ballad of Jake Brakes, published in The Great American Poetry Show, Vol. 3, 2015, and The Way to Reznicek's Farm, winner of a narrative poetry contest sponsored by the Kansas Author's Club. Based on experiences as a teacher of Tai Chi He has written two articles for Tai Chi Magazine, "Back to the Stable Syndrome," Vol. 34, No. 2, Summer 2010, and "Making Tai Chi Accessible to the Disabled" Vol. 36, No. 3, Fall 2012. David Hann has been a community volunteer for several years at the Lawrence Public Library and the Social Service League of Lawrence.

The author began writing what may be called biographical nonfiction after recording several stories told to him by great uncles and other relatives, initially transcribed for family members. Encouraged to write about his own experiences, he did that and acquired more biographical nonfiction from interviewing people whose stories intrigued him. These come together in Bluebirds to Tikal and other stories.

David lives in Lawrence, Kansas with his wife, Rose and two cats

Other Books You Might Enjoy From Anamcara Press

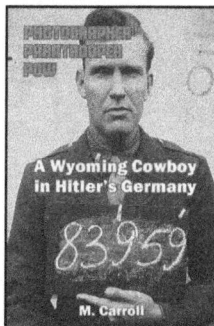

www.ingramcontent.com/pod-product-compliance
Lightning Source LLC
Chambersburg PA
CBHW022050020426
42335CB00012B/631